Low Fat
Low Carb

Everyday Cookery

D1148201

STAR
FIRE

This is a Starfire book
First published in 2005

05 07 09 08 06

3 5 7 9 10 8 6 4 2

Starfire is part of
The Foundry Creative Media Company Limited
Crabtree Hall, Crabtree Lane, Fulham, London, SW6 6TY

Visit our website: www.star-fire.co.uk

Copyright © The Foundry 2005

All rights reserved. No part of this publication may be reproduced, stored in a retrieval system
or transmitted, in any form or by any means, electronic, mechanical, photocopying, recording
or otherwise, without the prior permission of the copyright holder.

ISBN: 1-84451-308-4

The CIP record for this book is available from the British Library.

Printed in China

ACKNOWLEDGEMENTS

Publisher and Creative Director: Nick Wells
Project Editor and Editorial: Sarah Goulding
Design and Production: Chris Herbert, Mike Spender, Colin Rudderham and Claire Walker

Authors: Catherine Atkinson, Juliet Barker, Gina Steer, Vicki Smallwood,
Carol Tennant, Mari Mererid Williams, Elizabeth Wolf-Cohen and Simone Wright
Editorial: Gina Steer and Karen Fitzpatrick
Photography: Colin Bowling, Paul Forrester and Stephen Brayne
Home Economists and Stylists: Jacqueline Bellefontaine,
Mandy Phipps, Vicki Smallwood and Penny Stephens
Design Team: Helen Courtney, Jennifer Bishop, Lucy Bradbury and Chris Herbert

All props supplied by Barbara Stewart at Surfaces

NOTE
Recipes using uncooked eggs should be avoided by infants,
the elderly, pregnant women and anyone suffering from an illness.

Contents

Low Carb

Fish & Seafood

Poultry

Meat

Vegetables & Salads

Low Fat

Fish & Seafood

Poultry

Meat

Vegetables & Salads

Puddings & Desserts

Hygiene in the Kitchen

It is important to remember that many foods can carry some form of bacteria. In most cases, the worst it will lead to is a bout of food poisoning or gastroenteritis, although for certain people this can be serious. The risk can be reduced or eliminated, however, by good hygiene and proper cooking.

Do not buy food that is past its sell-by date and do not consume food that is past its use-by date. When buying food, use the eyes and nose. If the food looks tired, limp or a bad colour or it has a rank, acrid or simply bad smell, do not buy or eat it under any circumstances.

Take special care when preparing raw meat and fish. A separate chopping board should be used for each, and the knife, board and your hands should be thoroughly washed before handling or preparing any other food.

Regularly clean, defrost and clear out the refrigerator or freezer – it is worth checking the packaging to see exactly how long each product is safe to freeze. Avoid handling food if suffering from an upset stomach as bacteria can be

passed on through food preparation.

Dish cloths and tea towels must be washed and changed regularly. Ideally use disposable cloths which should be replaced on a daily basis. More durable cloths should be left to soak in bleach, then washed in the washing machine at a high temperature.

Keep your hands, cooking utensils and food preparation surfaces clean and do not allow pets to climb on to any work surfaces.

Buying

Avoid bulk buying where possible, especially fresh produce such as meat, poultry, fish, fruit and vegetables. Fresh foods lose their nutritional value rapidly, so buying a little at a time minimises loss of nutrients. It also means your fridge won't be so full, which reduces the effectiveness of the refrigeration process.

When buying prepackaged goods such as cans or pots of cream and yogurts, check that the packaging is intact and not damaged or pierced at all. Cans should not be dented, pierced or rusty. Check the sell-by dates even for cans and packets of dry ingredients such as flour and rice. Store fresh foods in the refrigerator as soon as possible – not in the car or the office.

When buying frozen foods, ensure that they are not heavily iced on the outside and that the contents feel completely frozen. Ensure that the frozen foods have been stored in the cabinet at the correct storage level and the temperature is below -18°C/ -0.4°F. Pack in cool bags to transport home and place in the freezer as soon as possible after purchase.

Preparation

Make sure that all work surfaces and utensils are clean and dry. Hygiene should be given priority at all times. Separate chopping boards should be used for raw and cooked

meats, fish and vegetables. Currently, a variety of good quality plastic boards come in various designs and colours. This makes differentiating easier and the plastic has the added hygienic advantage of being washable at high temperatures in the dishwasher. If using the board for fish, first wash in cold water, then in hot to prevent odour. Also remember that knives and utensils should always be thoroughly cleaned after use.

When cooking, be particularly careful to keep cooked and raw food separate to avoid any contamination. It is worth washing all fruits and vegetables regardless of whether they are going to be eaten raw or lightly cooked. This rule should apply even to prewashed herbs and salads.

Do not reheat food more than once. If using a microwave, always check that the food is piping hot all the way through – in theory, the food should reach 70°C/158°F and needs to be cooked at that temperature for at least three minutes to ensure that all bacteria are killed.

All poultry must be thoroughly thawed before using, including chicken and poussin. Remove the food to be thawed from the freezer and place in a shallow dish to contain the juices. Leave the food in the refrigerator until it is completely thawed. A 1.4 kg/3 lb whole chicken will take about 26–30 hours to thaw. To speed up the process, immerse the chicken in cold water, making sure that the water is changed regularly. When the joints can move freely and no ice crystals remain in the cavity, the bird is completely thawed.

Once thawed, remove the wrapper and pat the chicken dry. Place the chicken in a shallow dish, cover lightly and store as close to the base of the refrigerator as possible. The chicken should be cooked as soon as possible.

Some foods can be cooked from

frozen including many prepacked foods such as soups, sauces, casseroles and breads. Where applicable follow the manufacturers' instructions.

Vegetables and fruits can also be cooked from frozen, but meats and fish should be thawed first. The only time food can be refrozen is when the food has been thoroughly thawed then cooked. Once the food has cooled then it can be frozen again, but it should only be stored for one month.

All poultry and game (except for duck) must be cooked thoroughly. When cooked, the juices will run clear on the thickest part of the bird – the best area to try is usually the thigh. Other meats, like minced meat and pork should be cooked right the way through. Fish should turn opaque, be firm in texture and break easily into large flakes.

When cooking leftovers, make sure they are reheated until piping hot and that any sauce or soup reaches boiling point first.

Storing, Refrigerating and Freezing

Meat, poultry, fish, seafood and dairy products should all be refrigerated. The temperature of the refrigerator should be between 1–5°C/34–41°F while the freezer temperature should not rise above -18°C/-0.4°F.

To ensure the optimum refrigerator and freezer temperature, avoid leaving the door open for long periods of time. Try not to overstock the refrigerator as this reduces the airflow inside and therefore the effectiveness in cooling the food within.

When refrigerating cooked food, allow it to cool down quickly and completely before refrigerating. Hot food will raise the temperature of the refrigerator and possibly affect or spoil other food stored in it.

Food within the refrigerator and freezer should always be covered. Raw and cooked food should be stored in separate parts of the refrigerator. Cooked food should be kept on the top shelves of the refrigerator, while raw meat, poultry and fish should be placed on bottom shelves to avoid

drips and cross-contamination. It is recommended that eggs should be refrigerated in order to maintain their freshness and shelf life.

Take care that frozen foods are not stored in the freezer for too long. Blanched vegetables can be stored for one month; beef, lamb, poultry and pork for six months and unblanched vegetables and fruits in syrup for a year. Oily fish and sausages should be stored for three months. Dairy products can last four to six months, while cakes and pastries should be kept in the freezer for three to six months.

High Risk Foods

Certain foods may carry risks to people who are considered vulnerable such as the elderly, the ill, pregnant women, babies, young infants and those suffering from a recurring illness.

It is advisable to avoid those foods listed below which belong to a higher-risk category.

There is a slight chance that some eggs carry the bacteria salmonella. Cook the eggs until both the yolk and the white are firm to eliminate this risk. Pay particular attention to dishes and products incorporating lightly cooked or raw eggs which should be eliminated from the diet. Hollandaise sauce, mayonnaise, mousses, soufflés and meringues all use raw or lightly cooked eggs, as do custard-based dishes, ice creams and sorbets. These are all considered high-risk foods to the vulnerable groups mentioned above.

Certain meats and poultry also carry the potential risk of salmonella and so should be cooked thoroughly

until the juices run clear and there is no pinkness left. Unpasteurised products such as milk, cheese (especially soft cheese), pâté, meat (both raw and cooked) all have the potential risk of listeria and should be avoided.

When buying seafood, buy from a reputable source which has a high turnover to ensure freshness. Fish should have bright clear eyes, shiny skin and bright pink or red gills. The fish should feel stiff to the touch, with a slight smell of sea air and iodine. The flesh of fish steaks and fillets should be translucent with no signs of discolouration. Molluscs such as scallops, clams and mussels are sold fresh and are still alive. Avoid any that are open or do not close when tapped lightly. In the same way, univalves such as cockles or winkles should withdraw back into their shells when lightly prodded. When choosing cephalopods such as squid and octopus they should have a firm flesh and pleasant sea smell.

As with all fish, whether it is shellfish or seafish, care is required when freezing it. It is imperative to check whether the fish has been frozen before. If it has been frozen, then it should not be frozen again under any circumstances.

Nutrition The Role of Essential Nutrients

A healthy and well-balanced diet is the body's primary energy source. In children, it constitutes the building blocks for future health as well as providing lots of energy. In adults, it encourages self-healing and regeneration within the body. A well-balanced diet will provide the body with all the essential nutrients it needs. This can be achieved by eating a variety of foods, demonstrated in the pyramid below.

FATS

PROTEINS

milk,   meat, fish,
yogurt   poultry, eggs,
and cheese   nuts and pulses

FRUITS AND VEGETABLES

STARCHY CARBOHYDRATES
cereals, potatoes, bread, rice and pasta

FATS

Fats fall into two categories: saturated and unsaturated. It is very important that a healthy balance is achieved within the diet. Fats are an essential part of the diet: they are a source of energy and provide essential fatty acids and fat soluble vitamins. The right balance of fats should boost the body's immunity to infection and keep muscles, nerves and arteries in good condition. Saturated fats are of animal origin and are hard when stored at room temperature. They can be found in dairy produce, meat, eggs, margarines and hard white cooking fat (lard) as well as in manufactured products such as pies, biscuits and cakes. A high intake of saturated fat over many years has been proven to increase heart disease and high blood cholesterol levels and often leads to weight gain. The aim of a healthy diet is to keep the fat content low in the foods that we eat. Lowering the amount of saturated fat that we consume is very important, but this does not mean that it is good to consume lots of other types of fat.

There are two kinds of unsaturated fats: polyunsaturated and monounsaturated. Polyunsaturated fats include safflower, soybean, corn and sesame oils. Within the polyunsaturated group are Omega oils. The Omega-3 oils are of significant interest because they have been found to be particularly beneficial to coronary health and can encourage brain growth and development. Omega-3 oils are derived from oily fish such as salmon, mackerel, herring, pilchards and sardines. It is recommended that we should eat these types of fish at least once a week. However, for those who do not eat fish or who are vegetarians, liver oil supplements are available in most supermarkets and health shops. It is suggested that these supplements should be taken on a daily basis. The most popular oils that are high in monounsaturates are olive oil, sunflower oil and peanut oil. The Mediterranean diet which is based on a diet high in monounsaturated fats is recommended for heart health. Monounsaturated fats are also known to help reduce the levels of cholestrol.

PROTEINS

Composed of amino acids – proteins' building blocks – proteins perform a wide variety of essential functions for the body, including supplying energy and building and repairing tissues. Good sources of proteins are eggs, milk, yogurt, cheese, meat, fish, poultry, eggs, nuts and pulses. (See the second level of the pyramid.) Some of these foods, however, contain saturated fats. To strike a nutritional balance, eat generous amounts of vegetable protein foods such as soya, beans, lentils, peas and nuts.

FRUITS AND VEGETABLES

Not only are fruits and vegetables the most visually appealing foods, but they are extremely good for us, providing essential vitamins and minerals essential for growth, repair and protection in the human body. Fruits and vegetables are low in calories and are responsible for regulating the body's metabolic processes and controlling the composition of its fluids and cells.

MINERALS

CALCIUM Important for healthy bones and teeth, nerve transmission, muscle contraction, blood clotting and hormone function. Calcium promotes a healthy heart, improves skin, relieves aching muscles and bones, maintains the correct acid-alkaline balance and reduces menstrual cramps. Good sources are dairy products, small bones of small fish, nuts, pulses, fortified white flours, breads and green leafy vegetables.

CHROMIUM Part of the glucose tolerance factor, chromium balances blood sugar levels, helps to normalise hunger and reduce cravings, improves lifespan, helps protect DNA and is essential for heart function. Good sources are brewer's yeast, wholemeal bread, rye bread, oysters, potatoes, green peppers, butter and parsnips.

IODINE Important for the manufacture of thyroid hormones and for normal development. Good sources of iodine are seafood, seaweed, milk and dairy products.

IRON As a component of haemoglobin, iron carries oxygen around the body. It is vital for normal growth and development. Good sources are liver, corned beef, red meat, fortified breakfast cereals, pulses, green leafy vegetables, egg yolk, cocoa and cocoa products.

MAGNESIUM Important for efficient functioning of metabolic enzymes and development of the skeleton. Magnesium promotes healthy muscles by helping them to relax and is therefore good for PMS. It is also important for heart muscles and the nervous system. Good sources are nuts, green vegetables, meat, cereals, milk and yogurt.

PHOSPHORUS Forms and maintains bones and teeth, builds muscle tissue, helps maintain pH of the body and aids metabolism and energy production. Phosphorus is present in almost all foods.

POTASSIUM Enables nutrients to move into cells while waste products move out; promotes healthy nerves and muscles; maintains fluid balance in the body; helps secretion of insulin for blood sugar control to produce constant energy; relaxes muscles; maintains heart functioning and stimulates gut movement to encourage proper elimination. Good sources are fruit, vegetables, milk and bread.

SELENIUM Antioxidant properties help to protect against free radicals and carcinogens. Selenium reduces inflammation, stimulates the immune system to fight infections, promotes a healthy heart and helps vitamin E's action. It is also required for the male reproductive system and is needed for metabolism. Good sources are tuna, liver, kidney, meat, eggs, cereals, nuts and dairy products.

SODIUM Important in helping to control body fluid and balance, preventing dehydration. Sodium is involved in muscle and nerve function and helps move nutrients into cells. All foods are good sources. Processed, pickled and salted foods are richest in sodium but should be eaten in moderation.

ZINC Important for metabolism and the healing of wounds. It also aids ability to cope with stress, promotes a healthy nervous system and brain especially in the growing foetus, aids bone and teeth formation and is essential for constant energy. Good sources are liver, meat, pulses, whole-grain cereals, nuts and oysters.

VITAMINS

VITAMIN A Important for cell growth and developmemt and for the formation of visual pigments in the eye. Vitamin A comes in two forms: retinol and beta-carotenes. Retinol is found in liver, meat and meat products and whole milk and its products. Beta-carotene is a powerful antioxidant and is found in red and yellow fruits and vegetables such as carrots, mangoes and apricots.

VITAMIN B1 Important in releasing energy from carbohydrate-containing foods. Good sources are yeast and yeast products, bread, fortified breakfast cereals and potatoes.

VITAMIN B2 Important for metabolism of proteins, fats and carbohydrates to produce energy. Good sources are meat, yeast extracts, fortified breakfast cereals and milk and its products.

VITAMIN B3 Required for the metabolism of food into energy production. Good sources are milk and milk products, fortified breakfast cereals, pulses, meat, poultry and eggs.

VITAMIN B5 Important for the metabolism of food and energy production. All foods are good sources but especially fortified breakfast cereals, whole-grain bread and dairy products.

VITAMIN B6 Important for metabolism of protein and fat. Vitamin B6 may also be involved in the regulation of sex hormones. Good sources are liver, fish, pork, soya beans and peanuts.

VITAMIN B12 Important for the production of red blood cells and DNA. It is vital for growth and the nervous system. Good sources are meat, fish, eggs, poultry and milk.

BIOTIN Important for metabolism of fatty acids. Good sources of biotin are liver, kidney, eggs and nuts. Micro-organisms also manufacture this vitamin in the gut.

VITAMIN C Important for healing wounds and the formation of collagen which keeps skin and bones strong. It is an important antioxidant. Good sources are fruits, especially soft summer fruits, and vegetables.

VITAMIN D Important for absorption and handling of calcium to help build bone strength. Good sources are oily fish, eggs, whole milk and milk products, margarine and of course sufficient exposure to sunlight, as vitamin D is made in the skin.

VITAMIN E Important as an antioxidant vitamin helping to protect cell membranes from damage. Good sources are vegetable oils, margarines, seeds, nuts and green vegetables.

FOLIC ACID Critical during pregnancy for the development of the brain and nerves. It is always essential for brain and nerve function and is needed for utilising protein and red blood cell formation. Good sources are whole-grain cereals, fortified breakfast cereals, green leafy vegetables, oranges and liver.

VITAMIN K Important for controlling blood clotting. Good sources are cauliflower, Brussels sprouts, lettuce, cabbage, beans, broccoli, peas, asparagus, potatoes, corn oil, tomatoes and milk.

CARBOHYDRATES

Carbohydrates are an energy source and come in two forms: starch and sugar. Starch carbohydrates are also known as complex carbohydrates and they include all cereals, potatoes, breads, rice and pasta. (See the fourth level of the pyramid). Eating whole-grain varieties of these foods also provides fibre. Diets high in fibre are believed to be beneficial in helping to prevent bowel cancer and can also keep cholesterol down. High-fibre diets are also good for those concerned about weight gain. Fibre is bulky and fills the stomach, therefore reducing hunger pangs. Sugar carbohydrates which are also known as fast release carbohydrates because of the quick fix of energy they give to the body, and include sugar and sugar-sweetened products such as jams and syrups. Milk provides lactose which is a milk sugar and fruits provide fructose which is a fruit sugar.

Store Cupboard Essentials
Low–fat Ingredients for a Healthy Lifestyle

Low-fat cooking has often been associated with the stigma that reducing fat reduces flavour. This simply is not the case, which is great news for those choosing a lower-fat diet. Modern lifestyles are naturally shifting towards lower-fat and cholesterol diets, but there is no need to compromise on the choice of foods we eat thanks to the increasing number of lower-fat products now available in supermarkets.

The store cupboard is a good place to start when cooking low-fat meals. Most of us have fairly limited cooking and preparation time available during the week, so choose to experiment during weekends. When time is of the essence, or friends arrive unannounced, it is always a good idea, especially when following a low-fat diet, to have some well thought out basics in the cupboard: in particular, foods that are high on flavour and low in fat.

As store cupboard ingredients keep reasonably well, it really is worth making a trip to a good speciality grocery shop. Our society's growing obsession in recent years with travel and food from around the world has led us to seek out alternative ingredients with which to experiment and incorporate into our cooking. Consequently, supermarket chains have had to broaden their product range and often have a specialist range of imported ingredients from around the world.

If the grocers or local supermarket only carries a limited choice of products, do not despair. The internet now offers freedom to the food shopaholics amongst us. There are some fantastic food sites (both local and international) where food can be purchased and delivery arranged online.

When thinking about essentials, think of flavour, something that is going to add to a dish without increasing its fat content. It is worth spending a little bit more money on these products to make flavoursome dishes that will help stop the urge to snack on fatty foods.

Store cupboard hints

There are many different types of store cupboard ingredients readily available – including myriad varieties of rice and pasta – which can provide much of the carbohydrate required in our daily diets. Store the ingredients in a cool dark place and remember to rotate the store cupboard ingredients. The ingredients will be safe to use for at least six months.

BULGHUR WHEAT A cracked wheat which is often used in tabbouleh. Bulghur wheat is a good source of complex carbohydrate.

COUSCOUS Now available in instant form, couscous just needs to be covered with boiling water then forked. Couscous is a precooked wheat semolina. Traditional couscous needs to be steamed and is available from health food stores. This type of couscous contains more nutrients than the instant variety.

DRIED FRUIT The ready-to-eat variety are particularly good as they are plump, juicy and do not need to be soaked. They are fantastic when puréed into a compote, added to water and heated to make a pie filling and also when added to stuffing mixtures. They are also good cooked with meats, rice or couscous.

FLOURS A useful addition (particularly cornflour) which can be used to thicken sauces. It is worth mentioning that whole-grain flour should not be stored for too long at room temperature as the fats may turn rancid. While not strictly a flour, cornmeal is a very versatile low-fat ingredient, which can be used when making dumplings and gnocchi.

NOODLES Noodles are also very useful and can accompany any far-eastern dish. They are low-fat and also available in the wholewheat variety. Rice noodles are available for those who have gluten-free diets and, like pasta noodles, provide slow-release energy to the body.

PASTA It is good to have a mixture of wholewheat and plain pasta as well as a wide variety of flavoured pastas. Whether fresh (it can also be frozen) or dried, pasta is a versatile ingredient with which to provide the body with slow-release energy. It comes in many different sizes and shapes; from the tiny tubettini (which can be added to soups to create a more substantial dish), to penne, fusilli, rigatoni and conchiglie, up to the larger cannelloni and lasagne sheets.

POT AND PEARL BARLEY Pot barley is the complete barley grain whereas pearl barley has the outer husk removed. A high cereal diet can help to prevent bowel disorders and diseases.

PULSES A vital ingredient for the store cupboard, pulses are easy to store, have a very high nutritional value and are great when added to soups, casseroles, curries and hot pots. Pulses also act as a thickener, whether flavoured or on their own. They come in two forms; either dried (in which case they generally need to be soaked overnight and then cooked before use – it is important to follow the instructions on the back of the packet), or canned, which is a convenient timesaver because the preparation of dried pulses can take a while. If buying canned pulses, try to buy the variety in water with no added salt or sugar. These simply need to be drained and rinsed before being added to a dish. Kidney beans, borlotti, cannellini, butter, flageolet beans, split peas and lentils all make tasty additions to any dish. Baked beans are a favourite with everyone and many shops now stock the organic variety, which have no added salt or sugar but are sweetened with fruit juice instead.

When boiling previously dried pulses, remember that salt should not be added as this will make the skins tough and inedible. Puy lentils are a smaller variety. They often have mottled skins and are particularly good for cooking in slow dishes as they hold their shape and firm texture particularly well.

RICE Basmati and Thai fragrant rice are well suited to Thai and Indian curries as the fine grains absorb the sauce and their delicate creaminess balances the pungency of the spices. Arborio is only one type of risotto rice. Many are available depending on whether the risotto is meant to accompany meat, fish or vegetable dishes. When cooked, rice swells to create a substantial low-fat dish. Easy-cook American rice, both plain and whole-grain, is great for casseroles and for stuffing meat, fish and vegetables as it holds its shape and firmness. Pudding rice can be used in a variety of ways to create an irresistible dessert.

STOCK Good-quality stock is a must in low-fat cooking as it provides a good flavour base for many dishes. Many supermarkets now carry a variety of fresh and organic stocks that, although needing refrigeration, are probably one of the most time- and effort-saving ingredients available. There is also a fairly large range of dried stock, perhaps the best being bouillon, a high-quality form of stock (available in powder or liquid form) that can be added to any dish whether it be a sauce, casserole, pie or soup.

Many people favour meals which can be prepared and cooked in 30–45 minutes, so helpful ingredients which kick-start a sauce are great. A good-quality passata sauce or canned plum tomatoes can act as the foundation for any sauce, as can a good-quality green or red pesto. Other handy store cupboard additions include tapenade, mustard and anchovies. These ingredients have very distinctive t astes and are particularly flavoursome. Roasted red pepper sauce and sundried tomato purée, which tends to be sweeter and more intensely flavoured than regular tomato purée, are also very useful.

Vinegar is another worthwhile store cupboard essential and with so many uses it is worth splashing out on a really good-quality balsamic and wine vinegars. Herbs and spices are also a must. Using herbs when cooking at home should reduce the temptation to buy ready-made sauces, as often these types of sauces contain large amounts of sugar and additives.

Yeast extract is also a good store cupboard ingredient, which can pep up sauces, soups and casseroles and adds

a little substance, particularly to vegetarian dishes.

Eastern flavours offer a lot of scope where low-fat cooking is concerned. Flavourings such as fish sauce, soy sauce, red and green curry paste and Chinese rice wine all offer mouth-watering low-fat flavours to any dish.

For those who are incredibly short on time, or who rarely shop, it is now possible to purchase a selection of readily prepared freshly minced garlic, ginger and chilli. They are available in jars which can be kept in the refrigerator.

As well as these store cupboard additions, many shops and especially supermarkets provide a wide choice of products and carry a wide range of low-fat products. Where possible, invest in the leanest cut of meat and substitute saturated fats such as cream, butter and cheese with low-fat or half-fat alternatives, such as half-fat crème fraîche, fromage frais, butter and cheese.

Following a Low Carb Diet

Whether you're trying to lose weight, lower your cholesterol and blood pressure or you just want to improve your health and increase your energy levels, a low carbohydrate diet could be the answer. First developed in the 1970s, the low carb lifestyle has recently enjoyed a surge in interest that has in turn led to some health concerns regarding the possible long-term effects of following this diet. Although you should always consult your doctor before undertaking any weight loss programme, the recipes in this book have been especially chosen to help you enjoy a healthy diet without being too extreme. The recipes are not no carb, but low carb, and as such can fit in with your current diet to form part of a generally healthy lifestyle.

The basic principles of a low carb diet are to cut down, or cut out, the refined carbohydrates that lurk in processed and high sugar foods, bread, pasta, cereal and starchy vegetables such as potatoes. These are replaced with pure, lean proteins such as meat, fish, poultry, cheese, eggs and low sugar and low starch fruit and vegetables, including a limited amount of green vegetables. Most healthy diets advocate including carbohydrates in moderation, and it is important to note that most low carb diets instruct you to cut them out completely only for the first few weeks, gradually re-introducing them after this period.

The effectiveness of a low carb diet lies in how the body deals with fat and carbohydrates, two substances that most people's diets tend to be very high in these days, what with the huge popularity of fast food, takeaways and sweet snacks. The body burns up carbohydrates fairly easily, using them for energy. What happens on a low carb diet is that the body has no option but to start burning body fat, a state known as ketosis.

In addition, when you restrict your carbohydrate intake, your insulin levels decrease and the levels of glucagon increase. Glucagon is a hormone that causes body fat to be burned and cholesterol to be removed from deposits in the arteries. Therefore, if the body is trained to burn up fat first and carbohydrates second, a lot of weight can potentially be lost and healthy benefits gained. While the jury is still out regarding how healthy this is over the long term, it is generally agreed that a low carb, rather than a no carb, diet has health benefits that include a loss of weight and a reduction in cholesterol and blood pressure. Current guidelines suggest that on a healthy low carbohydrate diet, carbs should only make up around 5–10 per cent of your daily calorie intake. The recipes in this book aim to help strike this middle ground, allowing you to cut down on carbohydrates without jeopardising your future health, whilst also being straightforward and simple in order to fit into a busy life.

A low carb lifestyle is not for everyone, and trying some of these recipes may be a good way of judging whether it is a diet that you can stick to. If you are wanting to lose weight, you should be aware that not everyone loses the same amount of weight over the same period of time. Some people reach plateaus in their weight loss, while others can spend over a year

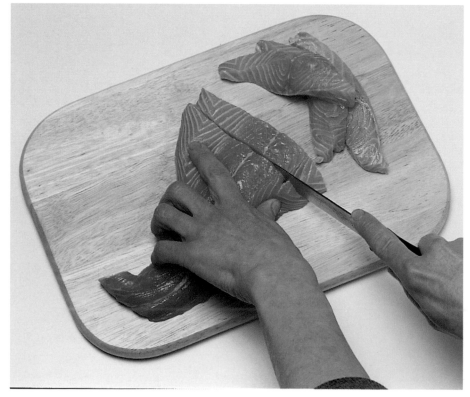

most large supermarkets. Restaurants and cafés have also noted the trend, and frequently offer low carb alternatives or adaptations to the food on offer.

Another advantage of the low carb diet, and one of the reasons for its current popularity, is the fact that only carbohydrates, not overall calories, need to be limited. You can eat as much as you want as often as you want, in order to prevent hunger, provided it is low in carbs. However, as with any diet, it is important to learn the distinction between being hungry and having an appetite. Genuine hunger means your body needs more food, so you need to eat. Having an appetite, on the other hand, is when you want to eat whether your body needs it or not. Learning to control these cravings and eating only when you are genuinely hungry is an important step to make when trying to lose weight. A low carb diet can be easier to stick to in this respect, as fats and oils, which are satisfying foods, are not seen as 'bad' and are therefore not restricted.

Perhaps one of the best pieces of dieting advice is 'everything in moderation', and if you are interested in discovering if the low carb lifestyle is for you, then this book is the perfect introduction.

losing weight gradually each week. The most recent scientific studies suggest that a low carb diet is safe and effective, however, and as well as the weight and health benefits, it can be good for helping to control diabetes. The very high protein content of a low carb diet means it is perhaps less suited to vegetarians and people who dislike too much meat in their diet, although several vegetarian dishes have been included here.

The main issue for most people wanting to try a low carb diet, however, is that cravings for foods such as pasta, pizza, bread and chocolate can be hard to overcome, but with more and more speciality low carb foods and products on the market, it is now relatively easy to find variety and stick to a low carb lifestyle. Everything from low carb chocolate bars and ice cream for satisfying a sweet tooth, to low carb pasta and beer are now available in

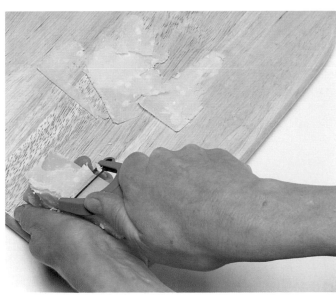

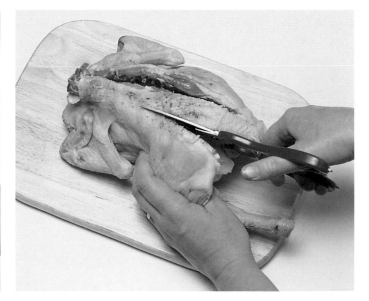

Low Carb

Seared Tuna with Italian Salsa

INGREDIENTS

Serves 4

4 x 175 g/6 oz tuna or
  swordfish steaks
salt and freshly ground black pepper
3 tbsp Pernod
2 tbsp olive oil
zest and juice of 1 lemon
2 tsp fresh thyme leaves
2 tsp fennel seeds, lightly roasted
4 sundried tomatoes, chopped
1 tsp dried chilli flakes
assorted salad leaves, to serve

For the salsa:

1 onion, peeled and finely chopped
2 tomatoes, deseeded and sliced
2 tbsp freshly shredded basil leaves
1 red chilli, deseeded and finely sliced
3 tbsp extra virgin olive oil
2 tsp balsamic vinegar

1 Wipe the fish and season lightly with salt and pepper, then place in a shallow dish. Mix together the Pernod, olive oil, lemon zest and juice, thyme, fennel seeds, sundried tomatoes and chilli flakes and pour over the fish. Cover lightly and leave to marinate in a cool place for 1–2 hours, occasionally spooning the marinade over the fish.

2 Meanwhile, mix all the ingredients for the salsa together in a small bowl. Season to taste with salt and pepper, then cover and leave for about 30 minutes to allow all the flavours to develop.

3 Lightly oil a griddle pan and place on the heat. When the pan is very hot, drain the fish, reserving the marinade. Cook the fish for 3–4 minutes on each side, taking care not to overcook it – the tuna steaks should be a little pink inside. Pour any remaining marinade into a small saucepan, bring to the boil and simmer for 1 minute. Serve the steaks hot with the marinade, chilled salsa and a few assorted salad leaves.

1

2

3

Roasted Cod with Saffron Aïoli

INGREDIENTS

Serves 4

For the saffron aïoli:

2 garlic cloves, peeled
¼ tsp saffron strands
sea salt, to taste
1 medium egg yolk
200 ml/7 fl oz extra virgin olive oil
2 tbsp lemon juice

For the marinade:

2 tbsp olive oil
4 garlic cloves, peeled and
  finely chopped
1 red onion, chopped
1 tbsp freshly chopped rosemary
2 tbsp freshly chopped thyme
4–6 sprigs of fresh rosemary
1 lemon, sliced

4 x 175 g/6 oz cod fillets with skin
freshly cooked vegetables, to serve

HELPFUL HINT

If you don't have time to prepare fresh aïoli, make the garlic and saffron paste as above and stir into a good quality bought mayonnaise.

1 Preheat the oven to 180°C/350°F/Gas Mark 4, 10 minutes before cooking. Crush the garlic, saffron and a pinch of salt with a pestle and mortar to form a paste. Place in a blender with the egg yolk and blend for 30 seconds. With the motor running, slowly add the olive oil in a thin, steady stream until the mayonnaise is smooth and thick. Spoon into a small bowl and stir in the lemon juice. Cover and leave in the refrigerator until required.

2 Combine the olive oil, garlic, red onion, rosemary and thyme for the marinade and leave to infuse for about 10 minutes.

3 Place the sprigs of rosemary and slices of lemon in the bottom of a lightly oiled roasting tin. Add the cod, skin-side up. Pour over the prepared marinade and leave to marinate in the refrigerator for 15–20 minutes.

4 Bake in the preheated oven for 15–20 minutes, or until the cod is cooked and the flesh flakes easily with a fork. Leave the cod to rest for 1 minute before serving with the saffron aïoli and vegetables.

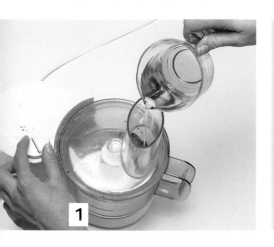

Seared Pancetta–wrapped Cod

INGREDIENTS

Serves 4

4 x 175 g/6 oz thick cod fillets
4 very thin slices of pancetta
3 tbsp capers in vinegar
1 tbsp of vegetable or sunflower oil
2 tbsp lemon juice
1 tbsp olive oil
freshly ground black pepper
1 tbsp freshly chopped parsley,
  to garnish
freshly cooked vegetables, to serve

1 Wipe the cod fillets and wrap each one with the pancetta. Secure each fillet with a cocktail stick and reserve.

2 Drain the capers and soak in cold water for 10 minutes to remove any excess salt, then drain again and reserve.

3 Heat the oil in a large frying pan and sear the wrapped pieces of cod fillet for about 3 minutes on each side, turning carefully with a fish slice so as not to break up the fish.

4 Lower the heat and continue to cook for 2–3 minutes or until the fish is thoroughly cooked.

5 Meanwhile, place the reserved capers, lemon juice and olive oil into a small saucepan. Grind over some black pepper.

6 Place the saucepan over a low heat and bring to a gentle simmer, stirring continuously for 2–3 minutes.

7 Once the fish is cooked, garnish with the parsley and serve with the warm caper dressing and freshly cooked vegetables.

HELPFUL HINT

As a delicious alternative to cod fillets, use salmon steaks. Great for when you're entertaining!

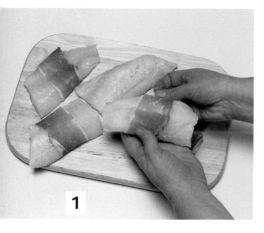

1

3

6

Mediterranean Fish Stew

INGREDIENTS

Serves 4–6

4 tbsp olive oil

1 onion, peeled and finely sliced

5 garlic cloves, peeled and
   finely sliced

1 fennel bulb, trimmed and
   finely chopped

3 celery sticks, trimmed and
   finely chopped

400 g can chopped tomatoes with
   Italian herbs

1 tbsp freshly chopped oregano

1 bay leaf

1 tsp saffron strands

750 ml/1¼ pints fish stock

3 tbsp dry vermouth

salt and freshly ground black pepper

225 g/8 oz thick haddock fillets

225 g/8 oz sea bass or bream fillets

225 g/8 oz raw tiger prawns, peeled

1 Heat the olive oil in a large saucepan. Add the onion, garlic, fennel and celery and cook over a low heat for 15 minutes, stirring frequently until the vegetables are soft and just beginning to turn brown.

2 Add the canned tomatoes with their juice, along with the oregano, bay leaf and saffron strands. Bring to the boil, then reduce the heat and simmer for 5 minutes. Add the fish stock and the vermouth and season to taste with salt and pepper. Bring to the boil. Reduce the heat and simmer for 20 minutes.

3 Wipe or rinse the haddock and bass fillets and remove as many of the bones as possible. Place on a chopping board and cut into 5 cm/2 inch cubes. Add to the saucepan and cook for 3 minutes, then add the prawns and cook for a further 5 minutes. Adjust the seasoning to taste and serve.

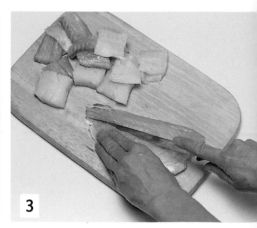

Citrus Monkfish Kebabs

INGREDIENTS

Serves 4

For the marinade:

1 tbsp sunflower oil
finely grated rind and juice of 1 lime
1 tbsp lemon juice
1 sprig of freshly chopped rosemary
1 tbsp wholegrain mustard
1 garlic clove, peeled and crushed
salt and freshly ground black pepper

For the kebabs:

450 g/1 lb monkfish tail
8 raw tiger prawns
1 small green courgette, trimmed
 and sliced
4 tbsp crème fraîche

HELPFUL HINT

Monkfish is very versatile. It can be roasted in the oven, poached, baked or grilled, and its firm flesh is ideal for kebabs.

1 Mix all the marinade ingredients together in a small bowl and reserve.

2 Using a sharp knife, cut down both sides of the monkfish tail. Remove the bone and discard. Cut away and discard any skin, then cut the monkfish into bite-sized cubes.

3 Peel the prawns, leaving the tails intact, and remove the thin black vein that runs down the back of each prawn. Place the fish and prawns in a shallow dish.

4 Pour the marinade over the fish and prawns. Cover lightly and leave to marinate in the refrigerator for 30 minutes. Spoon the marinade over the fish and prawns occasionally during this time. Soak the skewers in cold water for 30 minutes to stop them burning, then drain.

5 Preheat the grill and line the grill rack with tinfoil. Thread the cubes of fish, prawns and courgettes on to the drained skewers.

6 Arrange on the grill rack then place under the preheated grill and cook for 5–7 minutes, or until thoroughly cooked and the prawns have turned pink. Occasionally brush with the remaining marinade and turn the kebabs during cooking.

7 Mix 2 tablespoons of the marinade with the crème fraîche and serve as a dip with the kebabs.

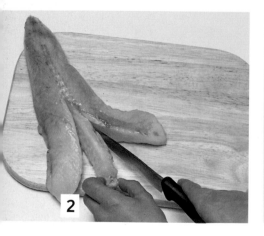

2

4

5

Fragrant Thai Swordfish with Peppers

INGREDIENTS

Serves 4–6

550 g/1¼ lb swordfish, cut into
   5 cm/2 inch strips
2 tbsp vegetable oil
2 lemon grass stalks, peeled, bruised
   and cut into 2.5 cm/1 inch pieces
2.5 cm/1 inch piece fresh root ginger,
   peeled and thinly sliced
4–5 shallots, peeled and thinly sliced
2–3 garlic cloves, peeled and
   thinly sliced
1 small red pepper, thinly sliced
1 small yellow pepper, thinly sliced
2 tbsp soy sauce
2 tbsp Chinese rice wine or dry sherry
1 tsp sesame oil
1 tbsp Thai or Italian basil, shredded
salt and black pepper
1 tbsp toasted sesame seeds

For the marinade:

1 tbsp soy sauce
1 tbsp Chinese rice wine or dry sherry
1 tbsp sesame oil

1 Blend all the marinade ingredients together in a shallow, non-metallic baking dish. Add the swordfish and spoon the marinade over the fish. Cover and leave to marinate in the refrigerator for at least 30 minutes.

2 Using a slotted spatula or spoon, remove the swordfish from the marinade and drain briefly on absorbent kitchen paper. Heat a wok or large frying pan, add the oil and, when hot, add the swordfish and stir-fry for 2 minutes, or until it begins to brown. Remove the swordfish and drain on absorbent kitchen paper.

3 Add the lemon grass, ginger, shallots and garlic to the wok and stir-fry for 30 seconds. Add the peppers, soy sauce, Chinese rice wine or sherry and stir-fry for 3–4 minutes.

4 Return the swordfish to the wok and stir-fry gently for 1–2 minutes, or until heated through and coated with the sauce. If necessary, moisten the sauce with a little of the marinade or some water. Stir in the sesame oil and the basil and season to taste with salt and pepper. Tip into a warmed serving bowl, sprinkle with sesame seeds and serve immediately.

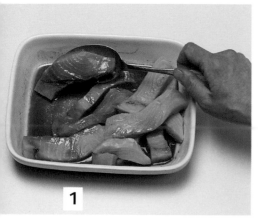

1

3

4

Fresh Tuna Salad

INGREDIENTS

Serves 4

225 g/8 oz mixed salad leaves

225 g/8 oz baby cherry tomatoes,
   halved lengthways

125 g/4 oz rocket leaves, washed

2 tbsp groundnut oil

550 g/1¼ lb boned tuna steaks, each
   cut into 4 small pieces

50 g/2 oz piece fresh
   Parmesan cheese

For the dressing:

8 tbsp olive oil

grated zest and juice of
   2 small lemons

1 tbsp wholegrain mustard

salt and freshly ground black pepper

1 Wash the salad leaves and place in a large salad bowl with the cherry tomatoes and rocket and reserve.

2 Heat the wok, then add the oil and heat until almost smoking. Add the tuna, skin-side down, and cook for 4–6 minutes, turning once during cooking. When the fish is cooked through and the flesh flakes easily, remove from the heat and leave to stand in the juices for 2 minutes before removing.

3 Meanwhile, to make the dressing, place the olive oil, lemon zest and juice and mustard in a small bowl or screw-topped jar and whisk or shake well until blended. Season to taste with salt and pepper.

4 Transfer the tuna to a clean chopping board and flake, then add it to the salad and toss lightly.

5 Using a swivel blade vegetable peeler, peel the piece of Parmesan cheese into shavings. Divide the salad between four large serving plates, drizzle the dressing over the salad, then scatter with the Parmesan shavings.

HELPFUL HINT

Bags of mixed salad leaves are available from all major super-markets. Although they seem expensive, there is very little waste and they do save time.

Prawn & Chilli Soup

INGREDIENTS

Serves 4

2 spring onions, trimmed
225 g/8 oz whole raw tiger prawns
750 ml/1¼ pint fish stock
finely grated rind and juice of 1 lime
1 tbsp fish sauce
1 red chilli, deseeded and chopped
1 tbsp soy sauce
1 lemon grass stalk
2 tbsp rice vinegar
4 tbsp freshly chopped coriander

1 To make spring onion curls, finely shred the spring onions lengthways. Place in a bowl of iced cold water and reserve.

2 Remove the heads and shells from the prawns, leaving the tails intact.

3 Split the prawns almost in two to form a butterfly shape and individually remove the black thread that runs down the back of each one.

4 In a large pan, heat the stock with the lime rind and juice, fish sauce, chilli and soy sauce.

5 Bruise the lemon grass by crushing it along its length with a rolling pin, then add to the stock mixture.

6 When the stock mixture is boiling, add the prawns and cook until they are pink.

7 Remove the lemon grass and add the rice vinegar and coriander.

8 Ladle into bowls and garnish with the spring onion curls. Serve immediately.

1

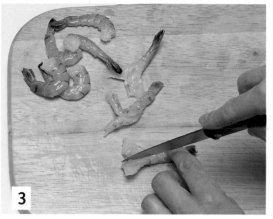

3

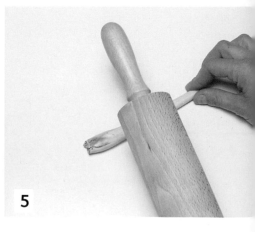

5

Teriyaki Salmon

INGREDIENTS

Serves 4

450 g/1 lb salmon fillet, skinned
6 tbsp Japanese teriyaki sauce
1 tbsp rice wine vinegar
1 tbsp tomato paste
dash of Tabasco sauce
grated zest of ½ lemon
salt and freshly ground black pepper
4 tbsp groundnut oil
1 carrot, peeled and cut
  into matchsticks
125 g/4 oz mangetout
125 g/4 oz oyster mushrooms, wiped

1 Using a sharp knife, cut the salmon into thick slices and place in a shallow dish. Mix together the teriyaki sauce, rice wine vinegar, tomato paste, Tabasco sauce, lemon zest and seasoning. Spoon the marinade over the salmon, then cover loosely and leave to marinate in the refrigerator for 30 minutes, turning the salmon or spooning the marinade occasionally over the fish.

2 Heat a large wok, then add 2 tablespoons of the oil until almost smoking. Stir-fry the carrot for 2 minutes, then add the mangetout and stir-fry for a further 2 minutes. Add the oyster mushrooms and stir-fry for 4 minutes, until softened. Using a slotted spoon, transfer the vegetables to four warmed serving plates and keep warm.

3 Remove the salmon from the marinade, reserving both the salmon and marinade. Add the remaining oil to the wok, heat until almost smoking, then cook the salmon for 4–5 minutes, turning once during cooking, or until the fish is just flaking. Add the marinade and heat through for 1 minute. Serve immediately, with the salmon arranged on top of the vegetables and the marinade drizzled over.

HELPFUL HINT

To make your own Teriyaki sauce, mix two tablespoons each of sake, mirin, Japanese soy sauce, and sugar. Beat together until the sugar has dissolved.

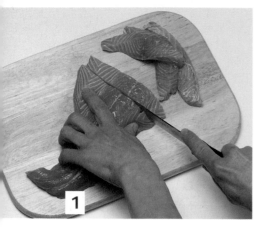

Thai Fish Cakes

INGREDIENTS

Serves 4

1 red chilli, deseeded and
   roughly chopped
4 tbsp roughly chopped
   fresh coriander
1 garlic clove, peeled and crushed
2 spring onions, trimmed and
   roughly chopped
1 lemon grass stalk, outer leaves
   discarded and roughly chopped
75 g/3 oz prawns, thawed if frozen
275 g/10 oz cod fillet, skinned, pin
   bones removed and cubed
salt and freshly ground black pepper
sweet chilli dipping sauce, to serve

HELPFUL HINT

A horseradish sauce could be
used in place of the sweet chilli
sauce if a creamier dip is
preferred. Mix 2 tbsp of grated
horseradish (from a jar) with 3
tbsp each of Greek yogurt and
mayonnaise. Add 3 finely chopped
spring onions, a squeeze of lime
and salt and pepper to taste.

1 Preheat the oven to 190°C/375°F/Gas Mark 5. Place the chilli, coriander, garlic, spring onions and lemon grass in a food processor and blend together.

2 Pat the prawns and cod dry with kitchen paper. Add to the food processor and blend until the mixture is roughly chopped.

3 Season to taste with salt and pepper and blend to mix.

4 Dampen your hands, then shape heaped tablespoons of the mixture into 12 little patties.

5 Place the patties on a lightly oiled baking sheet and cook in the preheated oven for 12–15 minutes or until piping hot and cooked through. Turn the patties over halfway through the cooking time.

6 Serve the fish cakes immediately with the sweet chilli sauce for dipping.

2

1

4

Creamy Caribbean Chicken & Coconut Soup

INGREDIENTS

Serves 4

4–6 spring onions

2 garlic cloves

1 red chilli

175 g/6 oz cooked chicken, shredded or diced

2 tbsp vegetable oil

1 tsp ground turmeric

300 ml/½ pint coconut milk

900 ml/1½ pints chicken stock

½ lemon, sliced

salt and freshly ground black pepper

1–2 tbsp freshly chopped coriander

sprigs of fresh coriander, to garnish

1 Trim the spring onions and thinly slice, then peel the garlic and finely chop. Cut off the top of the chilli, slit down the side and remove the seeds and membrane. Finely chop and reserve.

2 Remove and discard any skin or bones from the cooked chicken, shred using two forks and reserve.

3 Heat a large wok, add the oil and when hot add the spring onions, garlic and chilli and stir-fry for 2 minutes, or until the onion has softened. Stir in the turmeric and cook for 1 minute.

4 Blend the coconut milk with the chicken stock until smooth, then pour into the wok. Add the lemon slices and bring to the boil.

5 Simmer half-covered for 10 minutes, stirring occasionally.

6 Remove the lemon slices from the wok and add the chicken. Season to taste with salt and pepper and simmer for 2–3 minutes, or until the chicken is heated through thoroughly.

7 Stir in the chopped coriander and ladle into heated bowls. Garnish with sprigs of fresh coriander and serve immediately.

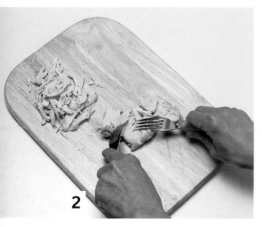

2

3

6

Chicken & Baby Vegetable Stir Fry

INGREDIENTS

Serves 4

2 tbsp groundnut oil

1 small red chilli, deseeded and finely chopped

150 g/5 oz chicken breast or thigh meat, skinned and cut into cubes

12 asparagus spears, halved

125 g/4 oz mangetout, trimmed

125 g/4 oz baby carrots, trimmed and halved lengthways

125 g/4 oz fine green beans, trimmed and diagonally sliced

125 g/4 oz baby sweetcorn, diagonally halved

50 ml/2 fl oz chicken stock

2 tsp light soy sauce

1 tbsp dry sherry

1 tsp sesame oil

toasted sesame seeds, to garnish

1 Heat the wok until very hot and add the oil. Add the chopped chilli and chicken and stir-fry for 4–5 minutes, or until the chicken is cooked and golden.

2 Increase the heat and add the asparagus spears, mangetout, baby carrots, green beans, and baby sweetcorn. Stir-fry for 3–4 minutes, or until the vegetables soften slightly but still retain a slight crispness.

3 In a small bowl, mix together the chicken stock, soy sauce, dry sherry and sesame oil. Pour into the wok, stir and cook until heated through.

4 Sprinkle with the toasted sesame seeds and serve immediately.

HELPFUL HINT

Look for packs of mixed baby vegetables in the supermarket. They are often available ready-trimmed and will save a lot of time.

Chicken Under a Brick

INGREDIENTS

Serves 4–6

1.8 kg/4 lb free range corn-fed,
   oven-ready chicken
50 ml/2 fl oz olive oil
sea salt and freshly ground
   black pepper

To garnish:

sprigs of fresh basil
chives

tossed bitter salad leaves, to serve

HELPFUL HINT

In a large bowl, whisk together 1 teaspoon of whole-grain mustard, 1 crushed garlic clove and 2 teaspoons of balsamic vinegar along with some salt and black pepper. When combined thoroughly, whisk in 3–4 tablespoons of some good quality olive oil to taste. Toss with a mixture of bitter leaves such as frisée, radicchio and chicory and serve with the chicken.

1   Rinse the chicken and dry well, inside and out. Using poultry shears or kitchen scissors, cut along each side of the backbone of the chicken and discard or use for stock. Place the chicken skin-side up on a work surface and, using the palm of your hand, press down firmly to break the breast bone and flatten the bird.

2   Turn the chicken breast-side up and use a sharp knife to slit the skin between the breast and thigh on each side. Fold the legs in and push the drumstick bones through the slits. Tuck the wings under, as the chicken should be as flat as possible.

3   Heat the olive oil in a large, heavy-based frying pan until very hot, but not smoking. Place the chicken in the pan skin-side down, and place a flat lid or plate directly on top of the chicken. Top with a brick (hence the name) or a 2 kg/5 lb weight. Cook for 12–15 minutes, or until golden brown.

4   Remove the weights and lid and, using a pair of tongs, turn the chicken carefully, then season to taste with salt and pepper. Cover and weight the lid again, then cook for 12–15 minutes longer, until the chicken is tender and the juices run clear when a thigh is pierced with a sharp knife or skewer.

5   Transfer the chicken to a serving plate and cover loosely with tinfoil to keep warm. Allow to rest for at least 10 minutes before carving. Garnish with sprigs of basil and chives and serve with salad leaves.

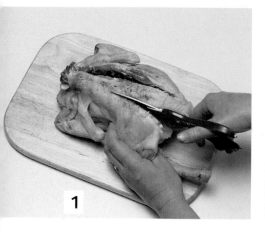

1

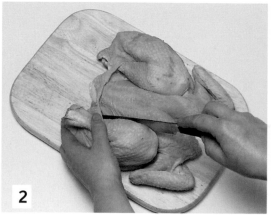

2

3

Garlic Mushrooms with Crispy Bacon & Chicken Liver Sauté

INGREDIENTS

Serves 4

4 large field mushrooms
40 g/1½ oz butter, melted and cooled
2 garlic cloves, peeled and crushed
1 tbsp sunflower oil
3 rashers smoked streaky bacon, rind
   removed and chopped
4 shallots, peeled and thinly sliced
450 g/1 lb chicken livers, halved
2 tbsp marsala or sweet sherry
4 tbsp chicken or vegetable stock
6 tbsp double cream
2 tsp freshly chopped thyme
salt and freshly ground black pepper

1. Remove the stalks from the mushrooms and roughly chop. Mix together 25 g/1 oz of the butter and garlic and brush over both sides of the mushroom caps. Place on the rack of a grill pan.

2. Heat a wok, add the oil and when hot, add the bacon and stir-fry for 2–3 minutes or until crispy. Remove and reserve. Add the remaining butter to the wok and stir-fry the shallots and chopped mushroom stalks for 4–5 minutes until they are softened.

3. Add the chicken livers and cook for 3–4 minutes, or until well browned on the outside, but still pink and tender inside. Pour in the marsala or sherry and the stock. Simmer for 1 minute, then stir in the cream, thyme, salt and pepper and half the bacon. Cook for about 30 seconds to heat through.

4. While the livers are frying, cook the mushroom caps under a hot grill for 3–4 minutes on each side, until tender.

5. Place the mushrooms on warmed serving plates, allowing one per person. Spoon the chicken livers over and around the mushrooms. Scatter with the remaining bacon and serve immediately.

1

2

3

Poached Chicken with Salsa Verde Herb Sauce

INGREDIENTS

Serves 6

6 boneless chicken breasts, each
  about 175 g/6 oz
600 ml/1 pint chicken stock,
  preferably homemade

For the salsa verde:

2 garlic cloves, peeled and chopped
4 tbsp freshly chopped parsley
3 tbsp freshly chopped mint
2 tsp capers
2 tbsp chopped gherkins (optional)
2–3 anchovy fillets in olive
  oil, drained and finely
  chopped (optional)
1 handful wild rocket leaves,
  chopped (optional)
2 tbsp lemon juice or red
  wine vinegar
125 ml/4 fl oz extra virgin olive oil
salt and freshly ground black pepper
sprigs of mint, to garnish

1 Place the chicken breasts with the stock in a large frying pan and bring to the boil. Reduce the heat and simmer for 10–15 minutes, or until cooked. Leave to cool in the stock.

2 To make the salsa verde, you need a food processor. Switch on the motor, then drop in the garlic cloves and chop finely. Add the parsley and mint and, using the pulse button, pulse 2–3 times. Add the capers and, if using, the gherkins, anchovies and rocket. Pulse 2–3 times until the sauce is evenly textured.

3 With the machine still running, pour in the lemon juice or red wine vinegar, then add the olive oil in a slow, steady stream until the sauce is smooth. Season to taste with salt and pepper, then transfer to a large serving bowl and reserve.

4 Carve each chicken breast into thick slices and arrange on serving plates, fanning out the slices slightly. Spoon over a little of the salsa verde on to each chicken breast, garnish with sprigs of mint and serve immediately with freshly cooked vegetables.

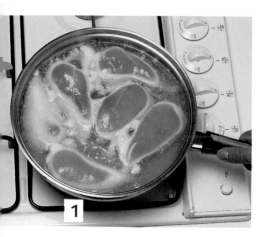

1

3

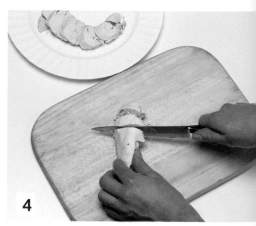

4

Turkey Escalopes Marsala with Wilted Watercress

INGREDIENTS

Serves 4

4 turkey breasts, each about
150 g/5 oz
½ tsp dried thyme
salt and freshly ground black pepper
1–2 tbsp olive oil
125 g/4 oz watercress
40 g/1½ oz butter
225 g/8 oz mushrooms, wiped
and quartered
50 ml/2 fl oz dry Marsala wine
50 ml/2 fl oz chicken stock or water

1 Place each piece of turkey between two sheets of non-stick baking paper and, using a meat mallet or rolling pin, pound to make an escalope about 3 mm/⅛ inch thick. Season each escalope with salt and pepper, sprinkle with dried thyme and reserve.

2 Heat the olive oil in a large frying pan, then add the watercress and stir-fry for about 2 minutes, until just wilted and brightly coloured. Season with salt and pepper. Using a slotted spoon, transfer the watercress to a plate and keep warm.

3 Add half the butter to the frying pan and, when melted, add the mushrooms. Stir-fry for 4 minutes, or until golden and tender. Remove from the pan and reserve. Add the remaining butter to the pan and, working in batches if necessary, cook the escalopes for 2–3 minutes on each side, or until golden and thoroughly cooked, adding the remaining oil if necessary. Remove from the pan and keep warm.

4 Add the Marsala wine to the pan and stir, scraping up any browned bits from the bottom of the pan. Add the stock or water and bring to the boil over a high heat. Season lightly. Return the escalopes and mushrooms to the pan and reheat gently until piping hot. Divide the warm watercress between four serving plates. Arrange 1 escalope over each serving of wilted watercress and spoon over the mushrooms and Marsala sauce. Serve immediately.

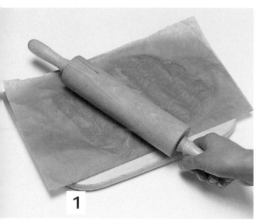

Lamb Meatballs with Savoy Cabbage

INGREDIENTS

Serves 4

450 g/1 lb fresh lamb mince
1 tbsp freshly chopped parsley
1 tbsp freshly grated root ginger
1 tbsp light soy sauce
1 medium egg yolk
4 tbsp dark soy sauce
2 tbsp dry sherry
3 tbsp vegetable oil
2 garlic cloves, peeled and chopped
1 bunch spring onions, trimmed
   and shredded
½ Savoy cabbage, trimmed
   and shredded
½ head Chinese leaves, trimmed
   and shredded
freshly chopped red chilli, to garnish

HELPFUL HINT

This dish is made with simple, basic ingredients, but you can substitute more Chinese ingredients if you prefer, such as rice wine vinegar instead of sherry and pak choi leaves instead of Savoy cabbage. As the meatballs contain raw egg, make sure that they are cooked thoroughly.

1 Place the lamb mince in a large bowl with the parsley, ginger, light soy sauce and egg yolk and mix together. Divide the mixture into walnut-sized pieces and, using your hands, roll into balls. Place on a baking sheet, cover with clingfilm and chill in the refrigerator for at least 30 minutes.

2 Meanwhile, blend together the dark soy sauce and sherry with 2 tablespoons of water in a small bowl. Reserve.

3 Heat a wok, add the oil and, when hot, add the meatballs. Cook for 5–8 minutes or until browned all over, turning occasionally. Using a slotted spoon, transfer the meatballs to a large plate and keep warm.

4 Add the garlic, spring onions, Savoy cabbage and the Chinese leaves to the wok and stir-fry for 3 minutes. Pour over the reserved soy sauce mixture, bring to the boil, then simmer for 30 seconds. Return the meatballs to the wok and mix in. Garnish with chopped red chilli and serve immediately.

1

3

4

Vitello Tonnato (Veal in Tuna Sauce)

INGREDIENTS

Serves 6–8

900 g/2 lb boned, rolled leg or
  loin of veal
300 ml/½ pint dry white wine
1 onion, peeled and chopped
2 celery stalks, trimmed and chopped
1 bay leaf
2 garlic cloves
few sprigs of parsley
salt and freshly ground black pepper
200 g can tuna in oil
2 tbsp capers, drained
6 anchovy fillets
200 ml/7 fl oz mayonnaise
juice of ½ lemon

To garnish:
lemon wedges
capers
black olives

To serve:
fresh green salad leaves
tomato wedges

1 Place the veal in a large bowl and pour over the wine. Add the onion, celery, bay leaf, garlic cloves, parsley, salt and pepper. Cover tightly and chill for 1 hour, or preferably overnight in the refrigerator. When needed, transfer the contents of the bowl to a large saucepan and add just enough water to cover the meat. Bring to the boil, cover and simmer for 1–1¼ hours, or until the veal is tender.

2 Remove from the heat and allow the veal to cool in the juices. Using a slotted spoon, transfer the veal to a plate, pat dry with absorbent kitchen paper and reserve.

3 Place the tuna, capers, anchovy fillets, mayonnaise and lemon juice in a food processor or liquidiser and blend until smooth, adding a few spoonfuls of the pan juices if necessary to make the sauce of a coating consistency. Season to taste with salt and pepper.

4 Using a sharp knife, slice the veal thinly and arrange on a large serving platter. Spoon the sauce over the veal. Garnish with lemon wedges, capers and olives and serve with salad and tomato wedges.

1

3

4

Chinese Leaf & Mushroom Soup

INGREDIENTS

Serves 4–6

450 g/1 lb Chinese leaves
25 g/1 oz dried Chinese
 (shiitake) mushrooms
1 tbsp vegetable oil
75 g/3 oz smoked streaky
 bacon, diced
2.5 cm/1 inch piece fresh root ginger,
 peeled and finely chopped
175 g/6 oz chestnut mushrooms,
 thinly sliced
1.1 litres/2 pints chicken stock
4–6 spring onions, trimmed and cut
 into short lengths
2 tbsp dry sherry or Chinese rice wine
salt and freshly ground black pepper
sesame oil for drizzling

1. Trim the stem ends of the Chinese leaves and cut in half lengthways. Remove the triangular core with a knife, then cut into 2.5 cm/1 inch slices and reserve.

2. Place the dried Chinese mushrooms in a bowl and pour over enough almost boiling water to cover. Leave to stand for 20 minutes to soften, then gently lift out and squeeze out the liquid. Discard the stems and thinly slice the caps and reserve. Strain the liquid through a muslin-lined sieve or a coffee filter paper and reserve.

3. Heat a wok over a medium-high heat, add the oil and when hot add the bacon. Stir-fry for 3–4 minutes, or until crisp and golden, stirring frequently. Add the ginger and chestnut mushrooms and stir-fry for a further 2–3 minutes.

4. Add the chicken stock and bring to the boil, skimming off any fat and scum that rises to the surface. Add the spring onions, sherry or rice wine, Chinese leaves, sliced Chinese mushrooms and season to taste with salt and pepper. Pour in the reserved soaking liquid and reduce the heat to the lowest possible setting.

5. Simmer gently, covered, until all the vegetables are very tender; this will take about 10 minutes. Add a little water if the liquid has reduced too much. Spoon into soup bowls and drizzle with a little sesame oil. Serve immediately.

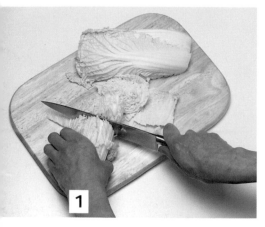

1

3

4

Aubergine Cannelloni with Watercress Sauce

INGREDIENTS

Serves 4

4 large aubergines, each about
  250 g/9 oz
5–6 tbsp olive oil
350 g/12 oz ricotta cheese
75 g/3 oz Parmesan cheese, grated
3 tbsp freshly chopped basil
salt and freshly ground black pepper
For the watercress sauce:
75 g/3 oz watercress, trimmed
200 ml/⅓ pint vegetable stock
1 shallot, peeled and sliced
pared strip of lemon rind
1 large sprig of thyme
3 tbsp crème fraîche
1 tsp lemon juice

To garnish:

sprigs of watercress
lemon zest

1. Preheat the oven to 190°C/375°F/Gas Mark 5, 10 minutes before cooking. Cut the aubergines lengthways into thin slices, discarding the side pieces. Heat 2 tablespoons of oil in a frying pan and cook the aubergine slices in a single layer in several batches, turning once, until golden on both sides.

2. Mix the cheeses, basil and seasoning together. Lay the aubergine slices on a clean surface and spread the cheese mixture evenly between them. Roll up the slices from one of the short ends to enclose the filling. Place, seam-side down, in a single layer in an ovenproof dish. Bake in the preheated oven for 15 minutes, or until golden.

3. To make the watercress sauce, blanch the watercress leaves in boiling water for about 30 seconds. Drain well, then rinse in a sieve under cold running water and squeeze dry. Put the stock, shallot, lemon rind and thyme in a small saucepan. Boil rapidly until reduced by half, then remove from the heat and strain.

4. Put the watercress and strained stock in a food processor and blend until fairly smooth. Return to the saucepan, stir in the crème fraîche, lemon juice and season to taste with salt and pepper. Heat gently until the sauce is piping hot. Serve a little of the sauce drizzled over the aubergines and the rest separately in a jug. Garnish the cannelloni with sprigs of watercress and lemon zest and serve immediately.

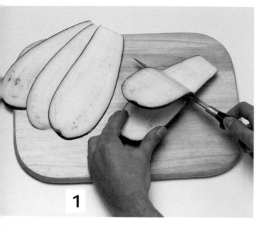

1

2

4

Bean & Cashew Stir Fry

INGREDIENTS

Serves 4

3 tbsp sunflower oil
1 onion, peeled and finely chopped
1 celery stalk, trimmed and chopped
2.5 cm/1 inch piece fresh root ginger,
   peeled and grated
2 garlic cloves, peeled and crushed
1 red chilli, deseeded and
   finely chopped
175 g/6 oz fine French beans,
   trimmed and halved
175 g/6 oz mangetout, sliced
   diagonally into 3
75 g/3 oz unsalted cashew nuts
125 ml/4 fl oz vegetable stock
2 tbsp dry sherry
1 tbsp light soy sauce
1 tsp red wine vinegar
salt and freshly ground black pepper
freshly chopped coriander, to garnish

1   Heat a wok or large frying pan, add the oil and when hot, add the onion and celery and stir-fry gently for 3–4 minutes or until softened.

2   Add the ginger, garlic and chilli to the wok and stir-fry for 30 seconds. Stir in the French beans and mangetout together with the cashew nuts and continue to stir-fry for 1–2 minutes, or until the nuts are golden brown.

3   Blend the stock with the sherry, soy sauce and vinegar. Stir into the bean mixture and bring to the boil. Simmer gently, stirring occasionally for 3–4 minutes, or until the beans and mangetout are tender but still crisp and the sauce has thickened slightly.

4   Season to taste with salt and pepper. Transfer to a warmed serving bowl or spoon on to individual plates. Sprinkle with freshly chopped coriander and serve immediately.

HELPFUL HINT

If you can get Chinese rice wine, or shaoxing, use this instead of the dry sherry.

Light Ratatouille

INGREDIENTS

Serves 4

1 red pepper

2 courgettes, trimmed

1 small aubergine, trimmed

1 onion, peeled

2 ripe tomatoes

50 g/2 oz button mushrooms, wiped
and halved or quartered

200 ml/7 fl oz tomato juice

1 tbsp freshly chopped basil

salt and freshly ground black pepper

1 Deseed the pepper and cut into small cubes. Thickly slice the courgettes and cut the aubergine into small cubes. Slice the onion into rings.

2 Place the tomatoes in boiling water until their skins begin to peel away. Remove the skins from the tomatoes, cut into quarters and remove the seeds.

3 Place all the vegetables in a saucepan with the tomato juice and basil. Season to taste with salt and pepper.

4 Bring to the boil, cover and simmer for 15 minutes or until the vegetables are tender.

5 Remove the vegetables with a slotted spoon and arrange in a serving dish.

6 Bring the liquid in the pan to the boil and boil for 20 seconds until it is slightly thickened. Season the sauce to taste with salt and pepper.

7 Pass the sauce through a sieve to remove some of the seeds and pour over the vegetables. Serve the ratatouille hot or cold.

1

3

5

Low Fat

Gingered Cod Steaks

INGREDIENTS

Serves 4

2.5 cm/1 inch piece fresh root
  ginger, peeled
4 spring onions
2 tsp freshly chopped parsley
1 tbsp soft brown sugar
4 x 175 g/6 oz thick cod steaks
salt and freshly ground black pepper
25 g/1 oz half-fat butter
freshly cooked vegetables, to serve

TASTY TIP

Why not serve this dish with roasted new potatoes *en papillote*? Place the new potatoes into double thickness greaseproof paper with a few cloves of peeled garlic. Drizzle with a little olive oil and season well with salt and black pepper. Fold all the edges of the greaseproof paper together and roast in the oven at 180°C/350°F/Gas Mark 4 for 40–50 minutes before serving in the paper casing.

1   Preheat the grill and line the grill rack with a layer of tinfoil. Coarsely grate the piece of ginger. Trim the spring onions and cut into thin strips.

2   Mix the spring onions, ginger, chopped parsley and sugar. Add 1 tablespoon of water.

3   Wipe the fish steaks. Season to taste with salt and pepper. Place on to 4 separate 20.5 x 20.5 cm/8 x 8 inch tinfoil squares.

4   Carefully spoon the spring onions and ginger mixture over the fish.

5   Cut the butter into small cubes and place over the fish.

6   Loosely fold the foil over the steaks to enclose the fish and to make a parcel.

7   Place under the preheated grill and cook for 10–12 minutes or until cooked and the flesh has turned opaque.

8   Place the fish parcels on individual serving plates. Serve immediately with the freshly cooked vegetables.

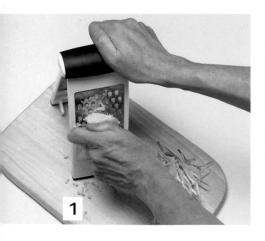

1

3

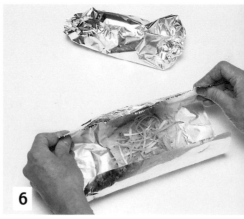

6

Mussels Linguine

INGREDIENTS

Serves 4

2 kg/4½ lb fresh mussels,
  washed and scrubbed
knob of butter
1 onion, peeled and finely chopped
300 ml/½ pint medium dry
  white wine

For the sauce:

1 tbsp sunflower oil
4 baby onions, peeled and quartered
2 garlic cloves, peeled and crushed
400 g can chopped tomatoes
large pinch of salt
225 g/8 oz dried linguine or tagliatelle
2 tbsp freshly chopped parsley

TASTY TIP

Serving mussels in their shells is a fantastic way to eat them. Every mussel is surrounded with the delicious sauce, adding flavour to every mouthful. Clams, which often have a sweeter flavour, could also be used in this recipe.

1 Soak the mussels in plenty of cold water. Leave in the refrigerator until required. When ready to use, scrub the mussel shells, removing any barnacles or beards. Discard any open mussels.

2 Melt the butter in a large pan. Add the mussels, onion and wine. Cover with a close-fitting lid and steam for 5–6 minutes, shaking the pan gently to ensure even cooking. Discard any mussels that have not opened, then strain and reserve the liquor.

3 To make the sauce, heat the oil in a medium-sized saucepan, and gently fry the quartered onion and garlic for 3–4 minutes until soft and transparent. Stir in the tomatoes and half the reserved mussel liquor. Bring to the boil and simmer for 7–10 minutes until the sauce begins to thicken.

4 Cook the pasta in boiling salted water for 7 minutes or or until 'al dente'. Drain the pasta, reserving 2 tablespoons of the cooking liquor, then return the pasta and liquor to the pan.

5 Remove the meat from half the mussel shells. Stir into the sauce along with the remaining mussels. Pour the hot sauce over the cooked pasta and toss gently. Garnish with the parsley and serve immediately.

Barbecued Fish Kebabs

INGREDIENTS

Serves 4

450 g/1 lb herring or mackerel fillets,
   cut into chunks
2 small red onions, peeled
   and quartered
16 cherry tomatoes
salt and freshly ground black pepper

For the sauce:
150 ml/¼ pint fish stock
5 tbsp tomato ketchup
2 tbsp Worcestershire sauce
2 tbsp wine vinegar
2 tbsp brown sugar
2 drops Tabasco
2 tbsp tomato purée

TASTY TIP

This dish would be ideal for the barbecue. Light it at least 20 minutes before use in order to allow the coals to heat up. The coals will have a grey-white ash when ready. Barbecue some peppers and red onions and serve with a mixed salad.

1 Line a grill rack with a single layer of tinfoil and preheat the grill at a high temperature, 2 minutes before use.

2 If using wooden skewers, soak in cold water for 30 minutes to prevent them from catching alight during cooking.

3 Meanwhile, prepare the sauce. Add the fish stock, tomato ketchup, Worcestershire sauce, vinegar, sugar, Tabasco and tomato purée to a small saucepan. Stir well and leave to simmer for 5 minutes.

4 When ready to cook, drain the skewers, if necessary, then thread the fish chunks, the quartered red onions and the cherry tomatoes alternately on to the skewers.

5 Season the kebabs to taste with salt and pepper and brush with the sauce. Grill under the preheated grill for 8–10 minutes, basting with the sauce occasionally during cooking. Turn the kebabs often to ensure that they are cooked thoroughly and evenly on all sides. Serve immediately with couscous.

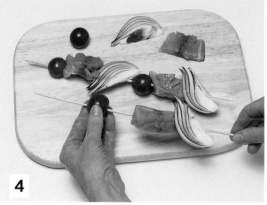

Ratatouille Mackerel

INGREDIENTS

Serves 4

1 red pepper
1 tbsp olive oil
1 red onion, peeled
1 garlic clove, peeled and thinly sliced
2 courgettes, trimmed and cut into
   thick slices
400 g can chopped tomatoes
sea salt and freshly ground
   black pepper
4 x 275 g/10 oz small mackerel,
   cleaned and heads removed
spray of olive oil
lemon juice for drizzling
12 fresh basil leaves
couscous or rice mixed with chopped
   parsley, to serve

1. Preheat the oven to 190°C/375°F/Gas Mark 5. Cut the top off the red pepper, remove the seeds and membrane, then cut into chunks. Cut the red onion into thick wedges.

2. Heat the oil in a large pan and cook the onion and garlic for 5 minutes or until beginning to soften.

3. Add the pepper chunks and courgettes slices and cook for a further 5 minutes.

4. Pour in the chopped tomatoes with their juice and cook for a further 5 minutes. Season to taste with salt and pepper and pour into an ovenproof dish.

5. Season the fish with salt and pepper and arrange on top of the vegetables. Spray with a little olive oil and lemon juice. Cover and cook in the preheated oven for 20 minutes.

6. Remove the cover, add the basil leaves and return to the oven for a further 5 minutes. Serve immediately with couscous or rice mixed with parsley.

FOOD FACT

Ratatouille is a traditional French dish using onions, tomatoes, courgettes and often aubergine. It is a very versatile dish to which many other vegetables can be added. For that extra kick, why not add a little chopped chilli.

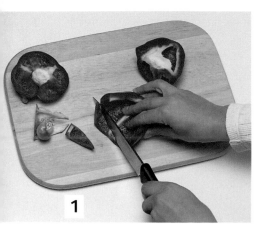

1

2

4

Cod with Fennel & Cardamom

INGREDIENTS

Serves 4

1 garlic clove, peeled and crushed
finely grated rind of 1 lemon
1 tsp lemon juice
1 tbsp olive oil
1 fennel bulb
1 tbsp cardamom pods
salt and freshly ground black pepper
4 x 175 g/6 oz thick cod fillets

FOOD FACT

When buying fresh fish, look for fish that does not smell. Any ammonia-type smelling fish should be avoided. The flesh should be plump and firm-looking. The eyes should be bright, not sunken. If in doubt, choose frozen fish. This is cleaned and packed almost as soon as it is caught. It is often fresher and contains more nutrients than its fresh counterparts.

1. Preheat the oven to 190°C/375°F/Gas Mark 5. Place the garlic in a small bowl with the lemon rind, juice and olive oil and stir well.

2. Cover and leave to infuse for at least 30 minutes. Stir well before using.

3. Trim the fennel bulb, thinly slice and place in a bowl.

4. Place the cardamom pods in a pestle and mortar and lightly pound to crack the pods.

5. Alternatively place in a polythene bag and pound gently with a rolling pin. Add the crushed cardamom to the fennel slices.

6. Season the fish with salt and pepper and place on to 4 separate 20.5 x 20.5 cm/8 x 8 inch parchment paper squares.

7. Spoon the fennel mixture over the fish and drizzle with the infused oil.

8. Place the parcels on a baking sheet and bake in the preheated oven for 8–10 minutes or until cooked. Serve immediately in the paper parcels.

1

4

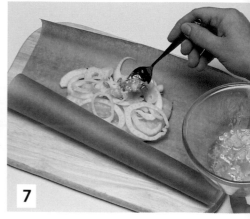
7

Haddock with an Olive Crust

INGREDIENTS

Serves 4

12 pitted black olives, finely chopped
75 g/3 oz fresh white breadcrumbs
1 tbsp freshly chopped tarragon
1 garlic clove, peeled and crushed
3 spring onions, trimmed and
  finely chopped
1 tbsp olive oil
4 x 175 g/6 oz thick skinless
  haddock fillets

To serve:
freshly cooked carrots
freshly cooked beans

TASTY TIP

Why not try experimenting by adding other ingredients to the crust? Adding 2 cloves of roasted garlic gives the crust a delicious flavour. Simply mash the garlic and add to the crumbs. Also, a combination of white and wholemeal breadcrumbs can be used for a nuttier, malty taste.

1 Preheat the oven to 190°C/375°F/Gas Mark 5. Place the black olives in a small bowl with the breadcrumbs and add the chopped tarragon.

2 Add the garlic to the olives with the chopped spring onions and the olive oil. Mix together lightly.

3 Wipe the fillets with either a clean damp cloth or damp kitchen paper, then place on a lightly oiled baking sheet.

4 Place spoonfuls of the olive and breadcrumb mixture on top of each fillet and press the mixture down lightly and evenly over the top of the fish.

5 Bake the fish in the preheated oven for 20–25 minutes or until the fish is cooked thoroughly and the topping is golden brown. Serve immediately with the freshly cooked carrots and beans.

2

3

4

Sardines with Redcurrants

INGREDIENTS

Serves 4

2 tbsp redcurrant jelly
finely grated rind of 1 lime
2 tbsp medium dry sherry
450 g/1 lb fresh sardines, cleaned
  and heads removed
sea salt and freshly ground
  black pepper
lime wedges, to garnish

To serve:
fresh redcurrants
fresh green salad

COOK'S TIP

Most fish are sold cleaned but it is easy to do yourself. Using the back of a knife, scrape off the scales from the tail towards the head. Make a small slit along their bellies using a sharp knife. Carefully scrape out the entrails and rinse thoroughly under cold running water. Pat dry with absorbent paper.

1 Preheat the grill and line the grill rack with tinfoil 2–3 minutes before cooking.

2 Warm the redcurrant jelly in a bowl standing over a pan of gently simmering water and stir until smooth. Add the lime rind and sherry to the bowl and stir well until blended.

3 Lightly rinse the sardines and pat dry with absorbent kitchen paper.

4 Place on a chopping board and with a sharp knife make several diagonal cuts across the flesh of each fish. Season the sardines inside the cavities with salt and pepper.

5 Gently brush the warm marinade over the skin and inside the cavities of the sardines.

6 Place on the grill rack and cook under the preheated grill for 8–10 minutes, or until the fish are cooked.

7 Carefully turn the sardines over at least once during grilling. Baste occasionally with the remaining redcurrant and lime marinade. Garnish with the redcurrants. Serve immediately with the salad and lime wedges.

2

4

5

Hot Salsa-filled Sole

INGREDIENTS

Serves 4

8 x 175 g/6 oz lemon sole
   fillets, skinned
150 ml/¼ pint orange juice
2 tbsp lemon juice

For the salsa:

1 small mango
8 cherry tomatoes, quartered
1 small red onion, peeled and
   finely chopped
pinch of sugar
1 red chilli
2 tbsp rice vinegar
zest and juice of 1 lime
1 tbsp olive oil
sea salt and freshly ground
   black pepper
2 tbsp freshly chopped mint
lime wedges, to garnish
salad leaves, to serve

HELPFUL HINT

Sometimes the skin will burn after handling chillies. Take care not to touch the eyes, before washing the hands.

1 First make the salsa. Peel the mango and cut the flesh away from the stone. Chop finely and place in a small bowl. Add the cherry tomatoes to the mango together with the onion and sugar.

2 Cut the top of the chilli. Slit down the side and discard the seeds and the membrane (the skin to which the seeds are attached). Finely chop the chilli and add to the mango mixture with the vinegar, lime zest, juice and oil. Season to taste with salt and pepper. Mix thoroughly and leave to stand for 30 minutes to allow the flavours to develop.

3 Lay the fish fillets on a board skinned side up and pile the salsa on the tail end of the fillets. Fold the fillets in half, season and place in a large shallow frying pan. Pour over the orange and lemon juice.

4 Bring to a gentle boil, then reduce the heat to a simmer. Cover and cook on a low heat for 7–10 minutes, adding a little water if the liquid is evaporating. Remove the cover, add the mint and cook uncovered for a further 3 minutes. Garnish with lime wedges and serve immediately with the salad.

1

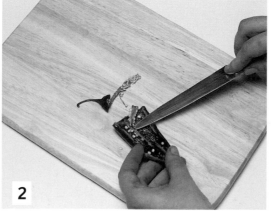

2

3

Scallops & Monkfish Kebabs with Fennel Sauce

INGREDIENTS

Serves 4

700 g/1½ lb monkfish tail
8 large fresh scallops
2 tbsp olive oil
1 garlic clove, peeled and crushed
freshly ground black pepper
1 fennel bulb, trimmed and
   thinly sliced
assorted salad leaves, to serve

For the sauce:

2 tbsp fennel seeds
pinch of chilli flakes
4 tbsp olive oil
2 tsp lemon juice
salt and freshly ground black pepper

1 Place the monkfish on a chopping board and remove the skin and the bone that runs down the centre of the tail and discard. Lightly rinse and pat dry with absorbent kitchen paper. Cut the 2 fillets into 12 equal-sized pieces and place in a shallow bowl.

2 Remove the scallops from their shells, if necessary, and clean thoroughly discarding the black vein. Rinse lightly and pat dry with absorbent kitchen paper. Put in the bowl with the fish.

3 Blend the 2 tablespoons of olive oil, the crushed garlic and a pinch of black pepper in a small bowl, then pour the mixture over the monkfish and scallops, making sure they are well coated. Cover lightly and leave to marinate in the refrigerator for at least 30 minutes, or longer if time permits. Spoon over the marinade occasionally.

4 Lightly crush the fennel seeds and chilli flakes in a pestle and mortar. Stir in the 4 tablespoons of olive oil and lemon juice and season to taste with salt and pepper. Cover and leave to infuse for 20 minutes.

5 Drain the monkfish and scallops, reserving the marinade and thread on to 4 skewers.

6 Spray a griddle pan with a fine spray of oil, then heat until almost smoking and cook the kebabs for 5–6 minutes, turning halfway through and brushing with the marinade throughout.

7 Brush the fennel slices with the fennel sauce and cook on the griddle for 1 minute on each side. Serve the fennel slices, topped with the kebabs and drizzled with the fennel sauce. Serve with a few assorted salad leaves.

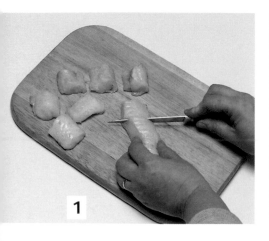

1

3

4

Smoked Haddock Rosti

INGREDIENTS

Serves 4

450 g/1 lb potatoes, peeled and
  coarsely grated
1 large onion, peeled and
  coarsely grated
2–3 garlic cloves, peeled and crushed
450 g/1 lb smoked haddock
1 tbsp olive oil
salt and freshly ground black pepper
finely grated rind of ½ lemon
1 tbsp freshly chopped parsley
2 tbsp half-fat crème fraîche
mixed salad leaves, to garnish
lemon wedges, to serve

1. Dry the grated potatoes in a clean tea towel. Rinse the grated onion thoroughly in cold water, dry in a clean tea towel and add to the potatoes.

2. Stir the garlic into the potato mixture. Skin the smoked haddock and remove as many of the tiny pin bones as possible. Cut into thin slices and reserve.

3. Heat the oil in a non-stick frying pan. Add half the potatoes and press well down in the frying pan. Season to taste with salt and pepper.

4. Add a layer of fish and a sprinkling of lemon rind, parsley and a little black pepper.

5. Top with the remaining potatoes and press down firmly. Cover with a sheet of tinfoil and cook on the lowest heat for 25–30 minutes.

6. Preheat the grill 2–3 minutes before the end of cooking time. Remove the tinfoil and place the rosti under the grill to brown. Turn out on to a warmed serving dish, and serve immediately with spoonfuls of crème fraîche, lemon wedges and mixed salad leaves.

HELPFUL HINT

Use smoked haddock fillets. Finnan or arbroath smokies would be too bony for this dish.

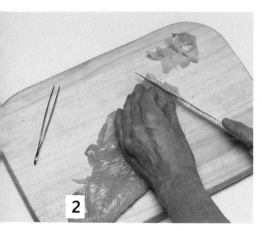

Sweet-&-Sour Prawns with Noodles

INGREDIENTS

Serves 4

425 g can pineapple pieces in
   natural juice
1 green pepper, deseeded and cut
   into quarters
1 tbsp groundnut oil
1 onion, cut into thin wedges
3 tbsp soft brown sugar
150 ml/ ¼ pint chicken stock
4 tbsp wine vinegar
1 tbsp tomato purée
1 tbsp light soy sauce
1 tbsp cornflour
350 g/12 oz raw tiger prawns, peeled
225 g/8 oz pak choi, shredded
350 g/12 oz medium egg noodles
coriander leaves, to garnish

HELPFUL HINT

This dish works well with Thai jasmine steamed rice and also wholewheat noodles which have more nutritional value. When using raw tiger prawns, make sure that the black vein that runs along their backs has been completely removed.

1 Make the sauce by draining the pineapple and reserving 2 tablespoons of the juice.

2 Remove the membrane from the quartered peppers and cut into thin strips.

3 Heat the oil in a saucepan. Add the onion and pepper and cook for about 4 minutes or until the onion has softened.

4 Add the pineapple, the sugar, stock, vinegar, tomato purée and the soy sauce.

5 Bring the sauce to the boil and simmer for about 4 minutes. Blend the cornflour with the reserved pineapple juice and stir into the pan, stirring until thickened.

6 Clean the prawns if needed. Wash the pak choi thoroughly, then shred.

7 Add the prawns and pak choi to the sauce. Simmer gently for 3 minutes or until the prawns are cooked and have turned pink.

8 Cook the noodles in boiling water for 4–5 minutes until just tender.

9 Drain and arrange the noodles on a warmed plate and pour over the sweet-and-sour prawns. Garnish with coriander leaves and serve immediately.

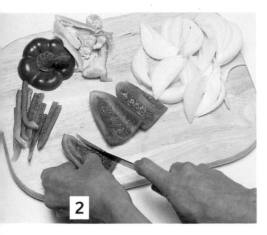

Sardines in Vine Leaves

INGREDIENTS

Serves 4

8–16 vine leaves in brine, drained
2 spring onions
6 tbsp olive oil
2 tbsp lime juice
2 tbsp freshly chopped oregano
1 tsp mustard powder
salt and freshly ground black pepper
8 sardines, cleaned
8 bay leaves
8 sprigs of fresh dill

To garnish:
lime wedges
sprigs of fresh dill

To serve:
olive salad
crusty bread

HELPFUL HINT

To clean sardines, first gut the fish. Insert a knife and make a cut along the belly. Remove the insides and discard. Wash the fish well. Remove the scales by gently rubbing your thumb along the fish from tail to head.

1   Preheat the grill and line the grill rack with tinfoil just before cooking. Cut 8 pieces of string about 25.5 cm/10 inches long, and leave to soak in cold water for about 10 minutes. Cover the vine leaves in almost boiling water. Leave for 20 minutes, then drain and rinse thoroughly. Pat the vine leaves dry with absorbent kitchen paper.

2   Trim the spring onions and finely chop, then place into a small bowl. With a balloon whisk beat in the olive oil, lime juice, oregano, mustard powder and season to taste with salt and pepper. Cover with clingfilm and leave in the refrigerator, until required. Stir the mixture before using.

3   Prepare the sardines, by making two slashes on both sides of each fish and brush with a little of the lime juice mixture. Place a bay leaf and a dill sprig inside each sardine cavity and wrap with 1–2 vine leaves, depending on size. Brush with the lime mixture and tie the vine leaves in place with string.

4   Grill the fish for 4–5 minutes on each side under a medium heat, brushing with a little more of the lime mixture if necessary. Leave the fish to rest, unwrap and discard the vine leaves. Garnish with lime wedges and sprigs of fresh dill and serve with the remaining lime mixture, olive salad and crusty bread.

1

3

3

Foil-baked Fish

INGREDIENTS

Serves 4

For the tomato sauce:

125 ml/4 fl oz olive oil

4 garlic cloves, peeled and
  finely chopped

4 shallots, peeled and finely chopped

400 g can chopped Italian tomatoes

2 tbsp freshly chopped
  flat-leaf parsley

3 tbsp basil leaves

salt and freshly ground black pepper

700 g/1½ lb red mullet, bass or
  haddock fillets

450 g/1 lb live mussels

4 squids

8 large raw prawns

2 tbsp olive oil

3 tbsp dry white wine

3 tbsp freshly chopped basil leaves

lemon wedges, to garnish

HELPFUL HINT

Make a large batch of sauce and keep covered in the refrigerator until needed or freeze for up to 2 months. Thaw completely and reheat gently before using.

1 Preheat oven to 180°C/350°F/Gas Mark 4, 10 minutes before cooking. Heat the olive oil and gently fry the garlic and shallots for 2 minutes. Stir in the tomatoes and simmer for 10 minutes, breaking the tomatoes down with the wooden spoon. Add the parsley and basil, season to taste with salt and pepper and cook for a further 2 minutes. Reserve and keep warm.

2 Lightly rinse the fish fillets and cut into four portions. Scrub the mussels thoroughly, removing the beard and any barnacles from the shells. Discard any mussels that are open. Clean the squid and cut into rings. Peel the prawns and remove the thin black intestinal vein that runs down the back.

3 Cut four large pieces of tinfoil, then place them on a large baking sheet and brush with olive oil. Place one fish portion in the centre of each piece of tinfoil. Close the tinfoil to form parcels. and bake in the preheated oven for 10 minutes, then remove.

4 Carefully open up the parcels and add the mussels, squid and prawns. Pour in the wine and spoon over a little of the tomato sauce. Sprinkle with the basil leaves and return to the oven and bake for 5 minutes, or until cooked thoroughly. Discard any unopened mussels, then garnish with lemon wedges and serve with the extra tomato sauce.

Mussels Arrabbiata

INGREDIENTS

Serves 4

1.8 kg/4 lb mussels

3–4 tbsp olive oil

1 large onion, peeled and sliced

4 garlic cloves, peeled and
   finely chopped

1 red chilli, deseeded and
   finely chopped

3 x 400 g cans chopped tomatoes

150 ml/¼ pint white wine

175 g/6 oz black olives, pitted
   and halved

salt and freshly ground black pepper

2 tbsp freshly chopped parsley

warm crusty bread, to serve

FOOD FACT

Arrabbiata sauce is a classic Italian tomato-based sauce, usually containing onions, peppers, garlic and fresh herbs. It needs slow simmering to bring out the flavour and is excellent with meat, poultry and pasta as well as seafood.

1 Clean the mussels by scrubbing with a small, soft brush, removing the beard and any barnacles from the shells. Discard any mussels that are open or have damaged shells. Place in a large bowl and cover with cold water. Change the water frequently before cooking and leave in the refrigerator until required.

2 Heat the olive oil in a large saucepan and sweat the onion, garlic and chilli until soft, but not coloured. Add the tomatoes and bring to the boil, then simmer for 15 minutes.

3 Add the white wine to the tomato sauce, bring the sauce to the boil and add the mussels. Cover and carefully shake the pan. Cook the mussels for 5–7 minutes, or until the shells have opened.

4 Add the olives to the pan and cook uncovered for about 5 minutes to warm through. Season to taste with salt and pepper and sprinkle in the chopped parsley. Discard any mussels that have not opened and serve immediately with lots of warm crusty bread.

Grilled Red Mullet with Orange & Anchovy Sauce

INGREDIENTS

Serves 4

2 oranges

4 x 175 g/6 oz red mullet, cleaned
   and descaled

salt and freshly ground black pepper

4 sprigs of fresh rosemary

1 lemon, sliced

2 tbsp olive oil

2 garlic cloves, peeled and crushed

6 anchovy fillets in oil, drained and
   roughly chopped

2 tsp freshly chopped rosemary

1 tsp lemon juice

1   Preheat the grill and line the grill rack with tinfoil just before cooking. Peel the oranges with a sharp knife, over a bowl in order to catch the juice. Cut into thin slices and reserve. If necessary, make up the juice to 150 ml/¼ pint with extra juice.

2   Place the fish on a chopping board and make two diagonal slashes across the thickest part of both sides of the fish. Season well, both inside and out, with salt and pepper. Tuck a rosemary sprig and a few lemon slices inside the cavity of each fish. Brush the fish with a little of the olive oil and then cook under the preheated grill for 4–5 minutes on each side. The flesh should just fall away from the bone.

3   Heat the remaining oil in a saucepan and gently fry the garlic and anchovies for 3–4 minutes. Do not allow to brown. Add the chopped rosemary and plenty of black pepper. The anchovies will be salty enough, so do not add any salt. Stir in the orange slices with their juice and the lemon juice. Simmer gently until heated through. Spoon the sauce over the red mullet and serve immediately.

HELPFUL HINT

Red mullet is a fairly common fish but size can vary enormously – often only very large fish are available. Substitute with grey mullet or snapper, if necessary.

1

2

3

Salmon Fish Cakes

INGREDIENTS

Serves 4

225 g/8 oz potatoes, peeled
450 g/1 lb salmon fillet, skinned
125 g/4 oz carrot, trimmed
  and peeled
2 tbsp grated lemon rind
2–3 tbsp freshly chopped coriander
1 medium egg yolk
salt and freshly ground black pepper
2 tbsp plain white flour
few fine sprays of oil

To serve:
prepared tomato sauce
tossed green salad
crusty bread

FOOD FACT

Salmon is now easily affordable due to salmon farming. It is readily available all year round and is often cheaper to buy than cod. It is an excellent source of Omega-3 fatty acids which help lower blood cholesterol levels.

1 Cube the potatoes and cook in lightly salted boiling water for 15 minutes. Drain and mash the potatoes. Place in a mixing bowl and reserve.

2 Place the salmon in a food processor and blend to form a chunky purée. Add the purée to the potatoes and mix together.

3 Coarsely grate the carrot and add to the fish with the lemon rind and the coriander.

4 Add the egg yolk, season to taste with salt and pepper, then gently mix the ingredients together. With damp hands form the mixture into four large fish cakes.

5 Coat in the flour and place on a plate. Cover loosely and chill for at least 30 minutes.

6 When ready to cook, spray a griddle pan with a few fine sprays of oil and heat the pan. When hot add the fish cakes and cook on both sides for 3–4 minutes or until the fish is cooked. Add an extra spray of oil if needed during the cooking.

7 When the fish cakes are cooked, serve immediately with the tomato sauce, green salad and crusty bread.

2

4

6

Citrus–grilled Plaice

INGREDIENTS

Serves 4

1 tsp sunflower oil
1 onion, peeled and chopped
1 orange pepper, deseeded
  and chopped
175 g/6 oz long-grain rice
150 ml/¼ pint orange juice
2 tbsp lemon juice
225 ml/8 fl oz vegetable stock
spray of oil
4 x 175 g/6 oz plaice fillets, skinned
1 orange
1 lemon
25 g/1 oz half-fat butter or
  low fat spread
2 tbsp freshly chopped tarragon
salt and freshly ground black pepper
lemon wedges, to garnish

TASTY TIP

Plaice is caught mainly from the North Sea and Icelandic waters. It can be bought, fresh or frozen, whole or in fillets and can be fried, poached or grilled. Dover or Lemon Sole or halibut can be used instead but they are more expensive to buy.

1   Heat the oil in a large frying pan, then sauté the onion, pepper and rice for 2 minutes.

2   Add the orange and lemon juice and bring to the boil. Reduce the heat, add half the stock and simmer for 15–20 minutes, or until the rice is tender, adding the remaining stock as necessary.

3   Preheat the grill. Finely spray the base of the grill pan with oil. Place the plaice fillets in the base and reserve.

4   Finely grate the orange and lemon rind. Squeeze the juice from half of each fruit.

5   Melt the butter or low-fat spread in a small saucepan. Add the grated rind, juice and half of the tarragon and use to baste the plaice fillets.

6   Cook one side only of the fish under the preheated grill at a medium heat for 4–6 minutes, basting continuously.

7   Once the rice is cooked, stir in the remaining tarragon and season to taste with salt and pepper. Garnish the fish with the lemon wedges and serve immediately with the rice.

2

4

5

Fish Lasagne

INGREDIENTS

Serves 4

75 g/3 oz mushrooms
1 tsp sunflower oil
1 small onion, peeled and
  finely chopped
1 tbsp freshly chopped oregano
400 g can chopped tomatoes
1 tbsp tomato purée
salt and freshly ground black pepper
450 g/1 lb cod or haddock
  fillets, skinned
9–12 sheets pre-cooked lasagne verde

For the topping:

1 medium egg, beaten
125 g/4 oz cottage cheese
150 ml/¼ pint low-fat natural yogurt
50 g/2 oz half-fat Cheddar
  cheese, grated

To serve:

mixed salad leaves
cherry tomatoes

1 Preheat the oven to 190°C/375°F/Gas Mark 5. Wipe the mushrooms, trim the stalks and chop. Heat the oil in a large heavy-based pan, add the onion and gently cook the onion for 3–5 minutes or until soft.

2 Stir in the mushrooms, the oregano and the chopped tomatoes with their juice.

3 Blend the tomato purée with 1 tablespoon of water. Stir into the pan and season to taste with salt and pepper.

4 Bring the sauce to the boil, then simmer uncovered for 5–10 minutes.

5 Remove as many of the tiny pin bones as possible from the fish and cut into cubes and add to the tomato sauce mixture. Stir gently and remove the pan from the heat.

6 Cover the base of an ovenproof dish with 2–3 sheets of the lasagne verde. Top with half of the fish mixture. Repeat the layers finishing with the lasagne sheets.

7 To make the topping, mix together the beaten egg, cottage cheese and yogurt. Pour over the lasagne and sprinkle with the cheese.

8 Cook the lasagne in the preheated oven for 40–45 minutes or until the topping is golden brown and bubbling. Serve the lasagne immediately with the mixed salad leaves and cherry tomatoes.

5

6

7

Fruits de Mer Stir Fry

INGREDIENTS

Serves 4

450 g/1 lb mixed fresh shellfish, such
   as tiger prawns, squid, scallops
   and mussels
2.5 cm/1 inch piece fresh root ginger
2 garlic cloves, peeled and crushed
2 green chillies, deseeded and
   finely chopped
3 tbsp light soy sauce
2 tbsp olive oil
200 g/7 oz baby sweetcorn, rinsed
200 g/7 oz asparagus tips, trimmed
   and cut in half
200 g/7 oz mangetout, trimmed
2 tbsp plum sauce
4 spring onions, trimmed and
   shredded, to garnish
freshly cooked rice, to serve

1 Prepare the shellfish. Peel the prawns and if necessary remove the thin black veins from the back of the prawns. Lightly rinse the squid rings and clean the scallops if necessary.

2 Remove and discard any mussels that are open. Scrub and debeard the remaining mussels, removing any barnacles from the shells. Cover the mussels with cold water until required.

3 Peel the root ginger and either coarsely grate or shred finely with a sharp knife and place into a small bowl.

4 Add the garlic and chillies to the small bowl, pour in the soy sauce and mix well.

5 Place the mixed shellfish, except the mussels in a bowl and pour over the marinade. Stir, cover and leave for 15 minutes.

6 Heat a wok until hot, then add the oil and heat until almost smoking. Add the prepared vegetables, stir-fry for 3 minutes, then stir in the plum sauce.

7 Add the shellfish and the mussels with the marinade and stir-fry for a further 3–4 minutes, or until the fish is cooked. Discard any mussels that have not opened. Garnish with the spring onions and serve immediately with the freshly cooked rice.

HELPFUL HINT

When stir-frying, it is important that the wok is heated before the oil is added. This ensures that that the food does not stick to the wok.

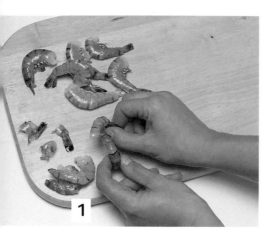

1

4

7

Zesty Whole–baked Fish

INGREDIENTS

Serves 8

1.8 kg/4 lb whole salmon, cleaned
sea salt and freshly ground black
  pepper
50 g/2 oz low-fat spread
1 garlic clove, peeled and finely sliced
zest and juice of 1 lemon
zest of 1 orange
1 tsp freshly grated nutmeg
3 tbsp Dijon mustard
2 tbsp fresh white breadcrumbs
2 bunches fresh dill
1 bunch fresh tarragon
1 lime sliced
150 ml/¼ pint half-fat crème fraîche
450 ml/¾ pint fromage frais
dill sprigs, to garnish

FOOD FACT

Wild salmon are normally caught
in the fresh waters of North
America and Northern Europe.
There are many varieties:
humpback (pink salmon), Chinook
and sockeye. Now that they are
farmed, they are more affordable.

1 Preheat the oven to 220°C/425°F/Gas Mark 7. Lightly rinse the fish and pat dry with absorbent kitchen paper. Season the cavity with a little salt and pepper. Make several diagonal cuts across the flesh of the fish and season.

2 Mix together the low-fat spread, garlic, lemon and orange zest and juice, nutmeg, mustard and fresh breadcrumbs. Mix well together. Spoon the breadcrumb mixture into the slits with a small sprig of dill. Place the remaining herbs inside the fish cavity. Weigh the fish and calculate the cooking time. Allow 10 minutes per 450 g/1 lb.

3 Lay the fish on a double thickness tinfoil. If liked, smear the fish with a little low fat spread. Top with the lime slices and fold the foil into a parcel. Chill in the refrigerator for about 15 minutes.

4 Place in a roasting tin and cook in the preheated oven for the calculated cooking time. Fifteen minutes before the end of cooking, open the foil and return until the skin begins to crisp. Remove the fish from the oven and stand for 10 minutes.

5 Pour the juices from the roasting tin into a saucepan. Bring to the boil and stir in the crème fraîche and fromage frais. Simmer for 3 minutes or until hot. Garnish with dill sprigs and serve immediately.

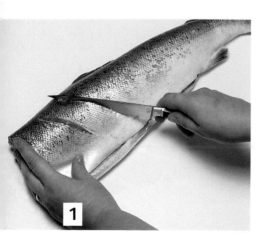

Seared Scallop Salad

INGREDIENTS

Serves 4

12 king (large) scallops
1 tbsp low-fat spread or butter
2 tbsp orange juice
2 tbsp balsamic vinegar
1 tbsp clear honey
2 ripe pears, washed
125 g/4 oz rocket
125 g/4 oz watercress
50 g/2 oz walnuts
freshly ground black pepper

FOOD FACT

As well as the king scallops which are used in this recipe, there are also the smaller queen scallops. It is worth noting that scallops are in season between September and March, when they will not only be at their best, but they may also be slightly cheaper in price. When buying, especially the larger king scallop, make sure that the orange roe is left intact.

1   Clean the scallops removing the thin black vein from around the white meat and coral. Rinse thoroughly and dry on absorbent kitchen paper.

2   Cut into 2–3 thick slices, depending on the scallop size.

3   Heat a griddle pan or heavy-based frying pan, then when hot, add the low-fat spread or butter and allow to melt.

4   Once melted, sear the scallops for 1 minute on each side or until golden. Remove from the pan and reserve.

5   Briskly whisk together the orange juice, balsamic vinegar and honey to make the dressing and reserve.

6   With a small, sharp knife carefully cut the pears into quarters, core then cut into chunks.

7   Mix the rocket leaves, watercress, pear chunks and walnuts. Pile on to serving plates and top with the scallops.

8   Drizzle over the dressing and grind over plenty of black pepper. Serve immediately.

1

4

6

Fish Roulades with Rice & Spinach

INGREDIENTS

Serves 4

4 x 175 g/6 oz lemon sole, skinned

salt and freshly ground black pepper

1 tsp fennel seeds

75 g/3 oz long-grain rice, cooked

150 g/5 oz white crab meat, fresh
   or canned

125 g/4 oz baby spinach, washed
   and trimmed

5 tbsp dry white wine

5 tbsp half-fat crème fraîche

2 tbsp freshly chopped parsley, plus
   extra to garnish

asparagus spears, to serve

FOOD FACT

Spinach is one of the healthiest, leafy green vegetables to be eaten. It also acts as an antioxidant and it is suggested that it can reduce risks of certain cancers. Why not use whole-grain rice to add nutritional value and to give the dish a nuttier taste.

1 Wipe each fish fillet with either a clean damp cloth or kitchen paper. Place on a chopping board, skinned side up and season lightly with salt and black pepper.

2 Place the fennel seeds in a pestle and mortar and crush lightly. Transfer to a small bowl and stir in the cooked rice. Drain the crab meat thoroughly. Add to the rice mixture and mix lightly.

3 Lay 2–3 spinach leaves over each fillet and top with a quarter of the crab meat mixture. Roll up and secure with a cocktail stick if necessary. Place into a large pan and pour over the wine. Cover and cook on a medium heat for 5–7 minutes or until cooked.

4 Remove the fish from the cooking liquor, and transfer to a serving plate and keep warm. Stir the crème fraîche into the cooking liquor and season to taste. Heat for 3 minutes, then stir in the chopped parsley.

5 Spoon the sauce on to the base of a plate. Cut each roulade into slices and arrange on top of the sauce. Serve with freshly cooked asparagus spears.

2

3

4

Griddled Garlic & Lemon Squid

INGREDIENTS

Serves 4

125 g/4 oz long-grain rice
300 ml/¹/₂ pint fish stock
225 g/8 oz squid, cleaned
finely grated rind of 1 lemon
1 garlic clove, peeled and crushed
1 shallot, peeled and finely chopped
2 tbsp freshly chopped coriander
2 tbsp lemon juice
salt and freshly ground black pepper

HELPFUL HINT

To prepare squid, peel the tentacles from the squid's pouch and cut away the head just below the eye. Discard the head. Remove the quill and the soft innards from the squid and discard. Peel off any dark skin that covers the squid and discard. Rinse the tentacles and pouch thoroughly. The squid is now ready to use.

1 Rinse the rice until the water runs clear, then place in a saucepan with the stock.

2 Bring to the boil, then reduce the heat. Cover and simmer gently for 10 minutes.

3 Turn off the heat and leave the pan covered so the rice can steam while you cook the squid.

4 Remove the tentacles from the squid and reserve.

5 Cut the body cavity in half. Using the tip of a small sharp knife, score the inside flesh of the body cavity in a diamond pattern. Do not cut all the way through.

6 Mix the lemon rind, crushed garlic and chopped shallot together.

7 Place the squid in a shallow bowl and sprinkle over the lemon mixture and stir.

8 Heat a griddle pan until almost smoking. Cook the squid for 3–4 minutes until cooked through, then slice.

9 Sprinkle with the coriander and lemon juice. Season to taste with salt and pepper. Drain the rice and serve immediately with the squid.

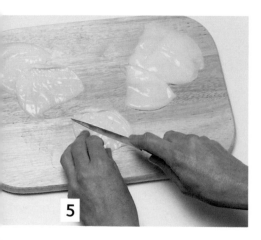

5

7

8

Smoked Salmon Sushi

INGREDIENTS

Serves 4

175 g/6 oz sushi rice
2 tbsp rice vinegar
4 tsp caster sugar
$\frac{1}{2}$ tsp salt
2 sheets sushi nori
60 g/2$\frac{1}{2}$ oz smoked salmon
$\frac{1}{4}$ cucumber, cut into fine strips

To serve:
wasabi
soy sauce
pickled ginger

TASTY TIP

If wasabi is unavailable, use a little horseradish. If unable to get sushi nori (seaweed sheets), shape the rice into small bite-size oblongs, then drape a piece of smoked salmon over each one and garnish with chives.

1 Rinse the rice thoroughly in cold water, until the water runs clear, then place in a pan with 300 ml/$\frac{1}{2}$ pint of water. Bring to the boil and cover with a tight-fitting lid. Reduce to a simmer and cook gently for 10 minutes. Turn the heat off, but keep the pan covered, to allow the rice to steam for a further 10 minutes.

2 In a small saucepan gently heat the rice vinegar, sugar and salt until the sugar has dissolved. When the rice has finished steaming, pour over the vinegar mixture and stir well to mix. Empty the rice out on to a large flat surface – a chopping board or large plate is ideal. Fan the rice to cool and to produce a shinier rice.

3 Lay one sheet of sushi nori on a sushi mat – if you do not have a sushi mat, improvise with a stiff piece of fabric that is a little larger than the sushi nori – and spread with half the cooled rice. Dampen the hands while doing this as it will help to prevent the rice from sticking to them. On the nearest edge place half the salmon and half the cucumber strips.

4 Roll up the rice and smoked salmon into a tight Swiss roll-like shape. Dampen the blade of a sharp knife and cut the sushi into slices about 2 cm/$\frac{3}{4}$ inch thick. Repeat with the remaining sushi nori, rice, smoked salmon and cucumber. Serve with wasabi, soy sauce and pickled ginger.

2

3

4

Honey & Ginger Prawns

INGREDIENTS

Serves 4

1 carrot

50 g/2 oz bamboo shoots

4 spring onions

1 tbsp clear honey

1 tbsp tomato ketchup

1 tsp soy sauce

2.5 cm/1 inch piece fresh root ginger,
  peeled and finely grated

1 garlic clove, peeled and crushed

1 tbsp lime juice

175 g/6 oz peeled prawns, thawed
  if frozen

2 heads little gem lettuce leaves

2 tbsp freshly chopped coriander

salt and freshly ground black pepper

To garnish:

fresh coriander sprigs

lime slices

HELPFUL HINT

If liked, raw tiger prawns can be used for this recipe – do make sure if using raw prawns that the black vein that runs along their back is removed.

1 Cut the carrot into matchstick-size pieces, roughly chop the bamboo shoots and finely slice the spring onions.

2 Combine the bamboo shoots with the carrot matchsticks and spring onions.

3 In a wok or large frying pan gently heat the honey, tomato ketchup, soy sauce, ginger, garlic and lime juice with 3 tablespoons of water. Bring to the boil.

4 Add the carrot mixture and stir-fry for 2–3 minutes until the vegetables are hot.

5 Add the prawns and continue to stir-fry for 2 minutes.

6 Remove the wok or frying pan from the heat and reserve until cooled slightly.

7 Divide the little gem lettuce into leaves and rinse lightly.

8 Stir the chopped coriander into the prawn mixture and season to taste with salt and pepper. Spoon into the lettuce leaves and serve immediately garnished with sprigs of fresh coriander and lime slices.

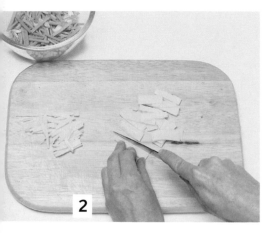

2

5

8

Chicken with Roasted Fennel & Citrus Rice

INGREDIENTS

Serves 4

2 tsp fennel seeds
1 tbsp freshly chopped oregano
1 garlic clove, peeled and crushed
salt and freshly ground black pepper
4 chicken quarters, about
   175 g/6 oz each
½ lemon, finely sliced
1 fennel bulb, trimmed
2 tsp olive oil
4 plum tomatoes
25 g/1 oz stoned green olives

To garnish:
fennel fronds
orange slices

For the citrus rice:
225 g/8 oz long-grain rice
finely grated rind and juice
   of ½ lemon
150 ml/¼ pint orange juice
450 ml/¾ pint boiling chicken or
   vegetable stock

1 Preheat the oven to 200°C/400°F/Gas Mark 6. Lightly crush the fennel seeds and mix with oregano, garlic, salt and pepper. Place between the skin and flesh of the chicken breasts, careful not to tear the skin. Arrange the lemon slices on top of the chicken.

2 Cut the fennel into 8 wedges. Place on baking tray with the chicken. Lightly brush the fennel with the oil. Cook the chicken and fennel on the top shelf of the preheated oven for 10 minutes.

3 Meanwhile, put the rice in a 2.3 litre/4 pint ovenproof dish. Stir in the lemon rind and juice, orange juice and stock. Cover with a lid and put on the middle shelf of the oven.

4 Reduce the oven temperature to 180°C/350°F/Gas Mark 4. Cook the chicken for a further 40 minutes, turning the fennel wedges and lemon slices once. Deseed and chop the tomatoes. Add to the tray and cook for 5–10 minutes. Remove from the oven.

5 When cooled slightly, remove the chicken skin and discard. Fluff the rice, scatter olives over the dish. Garnish with fennel fronds, orange slices and serve.

1

3

4

Chicken Baked in a Salt Crust

INGREDIENTS

Serves 4

1.8 kg/4 lb oven-ready chicken
salt and freshly ground black pepper
1 medium onion, peeled
sprig of fresh rosemary
sprig of fresh thyme
1 bay leaf
15 g/½ oz butter, softened
1 garlic clove, peeled and crushed
pinch of ground paprika
finely grated rind of ½ lemon

To garnish:
fresh herbs
lemon slices

For the salt crust:
900 g/2 lb plain flour
450 g/1 lb fine cooking salt
450 g/1 lb coarse sea salt
2 tbsp oil

HELPFUL HINT

It is best to avoid eating the skin from the chicken. It is high in fat and also absorbs a lot of salt from the crust.

1 Preheat the oven to 170°C/325°F/Gas Mark 3. Remove the giblets if necessary and rinse the chicken with cold water. Sprinkle the inside with salt and pepper. Put the onion inside with the rosemary, thyme and bay leaf.

2 Mix the butter, garlic, paprika and lemon rind together. Starting at the neck end, gently ease the skin from the chicken and push the mixture under.

3 To make the salt crust, put the flour and salts in a large mixing bowl and stir together. Make a well in the centre. Pour in 600 ml/1 pint of cold water and the oil. Mix to a stiff dough, then knead on a lightly floured surface for 2–3 minutes. Roll out the pastry to a circle with a diameter of about 51 cm/20 inches. Place the chicken breast side down in the middle. Lightly brush the edges with water, then fold over to enclose. Pinch the joints together to seal.

4 Put the chicken join-side down in a roasting tin and cook in the preheated oven for 2¾ hours. Remove from the oven and stand for 20 minutes.

5 Break open the hard crust and remove the chicken. Discard the crust. Remove the skin from the chicken, garnish with the fresh herbs and lemon slices. Serve the chicken immediately.

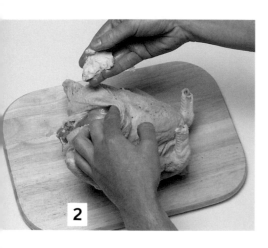
2

3

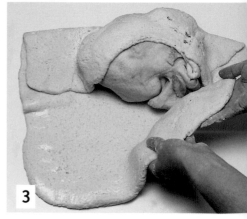
3

Spicy Chicken Skewers with Mango Tabbouleh

INGREDIENTS

Serves 4

400 g/14 oz chicken breast fillet
200 ml/7 fl oz natural low fat yogurt
1 garlic clove, peeled and crushed
1 small red chilli, deseeded and
   finely chopped
½ tsp ground turmeric
finely grated rind and juice
   of ½ lemon
sprigs of fresh mint, to garnish

For the mango tabbouleh:

175 g/6 oz bulgur wheat
1 tsp olive oil
juice of ½ lemon
½ red onion, finely chopped
1 ripe mango, halved, stoned, peeled
   and chopped
¼ cucumber, finely diced
2 tbsp freshly chopped parsley
2 tbsp freshly shredded mint
salt and finely ground black pepper

1 If using wooden skewers, pre-soak them in cold water for at least 30 minutes. (This stops them from burning during grilling.)

2 Cut the chicken into 5 x 1 cm/2 x ½ inch strips and place in a shallow dish.

3 Mix together the yogurt, garlic, chilli, turmeric, lemon rind and juice. Pour over the chicken and toss to coat. Cover and leave to marinate in the refrigerator for up to 8 hours.

4 To make the tabbouleh, put the bulgur wheat in a bowl. Pour over enough boiling water to cover. Put a plate over the bowl. Leave to soak for 20 minutes.

5 Whisk together the oil and lemon juice in a bowl. Add the red onion and leave to marinade for 10 minutes.

6 Drain the bulgur wheat and squeeze out any excess moisture in a clean tea towel. Add to the red onion with the mango, cucumber, herbs and season to taste with salt and pepper. Toss together.

7 Thread the chicken strips on to eight wooden or metal skewers. Cook under a hot grill for 8 minutes. Turn and brush with the marinade, until the chicken is lightly browned and cooked through.

8 Spoon the tabbouleh on to individual plates. Arrange the chicken skewers on top and garnish with the sprigs of mint. Serve warm or cold.

3

4

6

Pan-cooked Chicken with Thai Spices

INGREDIENTS

Serves 4

4 kaffir lime leaves
5 cm/2 inch piece of root ginger,
  peeled and chopped
300 ml/½ pint chicken stock, boiling
4 x 175 g/6 oz chicken breasts
2 tsp groundnut oil
5 tbsp coconut milk
1 tbsp fish sauce
2 red chillies, deseeded and
  finely chopped
225 g/8 oz Thai jasmine rice
1 tbsp lime juice
3 tbsp freshly chopped coriander
salt and freshly ground black pepper

To garnish:

wedges of lime
freshly chopped coriander

FOOD FACT

Fresh kaffir lime leaves can be found in Oriental food stores. Most supermarkets now stock dried kaffir lime leaves. If using dried, crumble lightly and use as above.

1 Lightly bruise the kaffir lime leaves and put in a bowl with the chopped ginger. Pour over the chicken stock, cover and leave to infuse for 30 minutes.

2 Meanwhile, cut each chicken breast into two pieces. Heat the oil in a large, non-stick frying pan or flameproof casserole and brown the chicken pieces for 2–3 minutes on each side.

3 Strain the infused chicken stock into the pan. Half cover the pan with a lid and gently simmer for 10 minutes.

4 Stir in the coconut milk, fish sauce and chopped chillies. Simmer, uncovered, for 5–6 minutes, or until the chicken is tender and cooked through and the sauce has reduced slightly.

5 Meanwhile, cook the rice in boiling salted water according to the packet instructions. Drain the rice thoroughly.

6 Stir the lime juice and chopped coriander into the sauce. Season to taste with salt and pepper. Serve the chicken and sauce on a bed of rice. Garnish with wedges of lime and freshly chopped coriander and serve immediately.

1

2

4

Sauvignon Chicken & Mushroom Filo Pie

INGREDIENTS

Serves 4

1 onion, peeled and chopped
1 leek, trimmed and chopped
225 ml/8 fl oz chicken stock
3 x 175 g/6 oz chicken breasts
150 ml/¹/₄ pint dry white wine
1 bay leaf
175 g/6 oz baby button mushrooms
2 tbsp plain flour
1 tbsp freshly chopped tarragon
salt and freshly ground black pepper
sprig of fresh parsley, to garnish
seasonal vegetables, to serve

For the topping:

75 g/3 oz (about 5 sheets) filo pastry
1 tbsp sunflower oil
1 tsp sesame seeds

1   Preheat the oven to 190°C/375°F/Gas Mark 5. Put the onion and leek in a heavy-based saucepan with 125 ml/4 fl oz of the stock.

2   Bring to the boil, cover and simmer for 5 minutes, then uncover and cook until all the stock has evaporated and the vegetables are tender.

3   Cut the chicken into bite-sized cubes. Add to the pan with the remaining stock, wine and bay leaf. Cover and gently simmer for 5 minutes. Add the mushrooms and simmer for a further 5 minutes.

4   Blend the flour with 3 tablespoons of cold water. Stir into the pan and cook, stirring all the time until the sauce has thickened.

5   Stir the tarragon into the sauce and season with salt and pepper.

6   Spoon the mixture into a 1.2 litre/2 pint pie dish, discarding the bay leaf.

7   Lightly brush a sheet of filo pastry with a little of the oil.

8   Crumple the pastry slightly. Arrange on top of the filling. Repeat with the remaining filo sheets and oil, then sprinkle the top of the pie with the sesame seeds.

9   Bake the pie on the middle shelf of the preheated oven for 20 minutes until the filo pastry topping is golden and crisp. Garnish with a sprig of parsley. Serve the pie immediately with the seasonal vegetables.

3

6

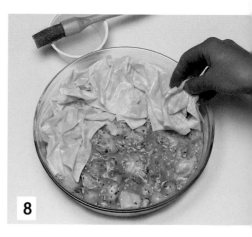

8

Chilli Roast Chicken

INGREDIENTS

Serves 4

3 medium-hot fresh red chillies,
   deseeded
½ tsp ground turmeric
1 tsp cumin seeds
1 tsp coriander seeds
2 garlic cloves, peeled and crushed
2.5 cm/1 inch piece fresh root ginger,
   peeled and chopped
1 tbsp lemon juice
1 tbsp olive oil
2 tbsp roughly chopped
   fresh coriander
½ tsp salt
freshly ground black pepper
1.4 kg/3 lb oven-ready chicken
15 g/½ oz unsalted butter, melted
550 g/1¼ lb butternut squash
fresh parsley and coriander sprigs, to
   garnish

To serve:

4 baked potatoes
seasonal green vegetables

1. Preheat the oven to 190°C/375°F/Gas Mark 5. Roughly chop the chillies and put in a food processor with the turmeric, cumin seeds, coriander seeds, garlic, ginger, lemon juice, olive oil, coriander, salt, pepper and 2 tablespoons of cold water. Blend to a paste, leaving the ingredients still slightly chunky.

2. Starting at the neck end of the chicken, gently ease up the skin to loosen it from the breast. Reserve 3 tablespoons of the paste. Push the remaining paste over the chicken breast under the skin, spreading it evenly.

3. Put the chicken in a large roasting tin. Mix the reserved chilli paste with the melted butter. Use 1 tablespoon to brush evenly over the chicken, roast in the preheated oven for 20 minutes.

4. Meanwhile, halve, peel and scoop out the seeds from the butternut squash. Cut into large chunks and mix in the remaining chilli paste and butter mixture.

5. Arrange the butternut squash around the chicken. Roast for a further hour, basting with the cooking juices about every 20 minutes until the chicken is fully cooked and the squash tender. Garnish with parsley and coriander. Serve hot with baked potatoes and green vegetables.

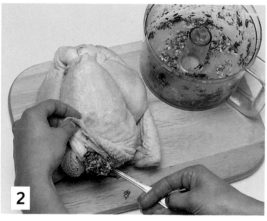

Aromatic Chicken Curry

INGREDIENTS

Serves 4

125 g/4 oz red lentils

2 tsp ground coriander

½ tsp cumin seeds

2 tsp mild curry paste

1 bay leaf

small strip of lemon rind

600 ml/1 pint chicken or
  vegetable stock

8 chicken thighs, skinned

175 g/6 oz spinach leaves, rinsed
  and shredded

1 tbsp freshly chopped coriander

2 tsp lemon juice

salt and freshly ground black pepper

To serve:

freshly cooked rice

low fat natural yogurt

HELPFUL HINT

Dry-frying spices really releases their flavour. It is a particularly good way to flavour lean meat or fish. Try mixing dry-fried spices with a little water or oil to make a paste. Apply the paste before baking to make a spicy crust.

1 Put the lentils in a sieve and rinse thoroughly under cold running water.

2 Dry-fry the ground coriander and cumin seeds in a large saucepan over a low heat for about 30 seconds. Stir in the curry paste.

3 Add the lentils to the saucepan with the bay leaf and lemon rind, then pour in the stock.

4 Stir, then slowly bring to the boil. Turn down the heat, half-cover the pan with a lid and simmer gently for 5 minutes, stirring occasionally.

5 Secure the chicken thighs with cocktail sticks to keep their shape. Place in the pan and half-cover. Simmer for 15 minutes.

6 Stir in the shredded spinach and cook for a further 25 minutes or until the chicken is very tender and the sauce is thick.

7 Remove the bay leaf and lemon rind. Stir in the coriander and lemon juice, then season to taste with salt and pepper. Serve immediately with the rice and a little natural yogurt.

Chicken Cacciatore

INGREDIENTS

Serves 4

4 chicken leg portions
1 tbsp olive oil
1 red onion, peeled and cut into very
  thin wedges
1 garlic clove, peeled and crushed
sprig of fresh thyme
sprig of fresh rosemary
150 ml/¼ pint dry white wine
200 ml/7 fl oz chicken stock
400 g can chopped tomatoes
40 g/1½ oz black olives, pitted
15 g/½ oz capers, drained
salt and freshly ground black pepper
freshly cooked fettuccine, linguine or
  pasta shells

HELPFUL HINT

When watching your saturated fat intake, it is essential to remove the skin from the chicken before eating. Any fat is deposited directly underneath the skin.

1 Skin the chicken portions and cut each one into 2 pieces to make 4 thighs and 4 drumsticks.

2 Heat 2 teaspoons of the oil in a flameproof casserole and cook the chicken for 2–3 minutes on each side until lightly browned. Remove the chicken from the pan and reserve.

3 Add the remaining 1 teaspoon of oil to the juices in the pan.

4 Add the red onion and gently cook for 5 minutes, stirring occasionally.

5 Add the garlic and cook for a further 5 minutes until soft and beginning to brown. Return the chicken to the pan.

6 Add the herbs, then pour in the wine and let it bubble for 1–2 minutes.

7 Add the stock and tomatoes, cover and gently simmer for 15 minutes.

8 Stir in the olives and capers. Cook uncovered for a further 5 minutes or until the chicken is cooked and the sauce thickened. Remove the herbs and season to taste with salt and pepper.

9 Place the chicken on a bed of pasta, allowing one thigh and one drumstick per person. Spoon over the sauce and serve.

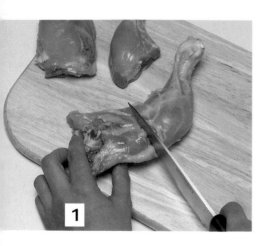

Chicken & Summer Vegetable Risotto

INGREDIENTS

Serves 4

1 litre/1³/₄ pint chicken or
  vegetable stock
225 g/8 oz baby asparagus spears
125 g/4 oz French beans
15 g/¹/₂ oz butter
1 small onion, peeled and
  finely chopped
150 ml/¹/₄ pint dry white wine
275 g/10 oz arborio rice
pinch of saffron strands
75 g/3 oz frozen peas, thawed
225 g/8 oz cooked chicken,
  skinned and diced
juice of ¹/₂ lemon
salt and freshly ground black pepper
25 g/1 oz Parmesan, shaved

1 Bring the stock to the boil in a large saucepan. Trim the asparagus and cut into 4 cm/1¹/₂ inch lengths.

2 Blanch the asparagus in the stock for 1–2 minutes or until tender, then remove with a slotted spoon and reserve.

3 Halve the green beans and cook in the boiling stock for 4 minutes. Remove and reserve. Turn down the heat and keep the stock barely simmering.

4 Melt the butter in a heavy-based saucepan. Add the onion and cook gently for about 5 minutes.

5 Pour the wine into the pan and boil rapidly until the liquid has almost reduced. Add the rice and cook, stirring for 1 minute until the grains are coated and look translucent.

6 Add the saffron and a ladle of the stock. Simmer, stirring all the time, until the stock has absorbed. Continue adding the stock, a ladle at a time, until it has all been absorbed.

7 After 15 minutes the risotto should be creamy with a slight bite to it. If not, add a little more stock and cook for a few more minutes, or until it is of the correct texture and consistency.

8 Add the peas, reserved vegetables, chicken and lemon juice. Season to taste with salt and pepper and cook for 3–4 minutes or until the chicken is thoroughly heated and piping hot.

9 Spoon the risotto on to warmed serving plates. Scatter each portion with a few shavings of Parmesan cheese and serve immediately.

Mexican Chicken

INGREDIENTS

Serves 4

1.4 kg/3 lb oven-ready
  chicken, jointed
3 tbsp plain flour
½ tsp ground paprika pepper
salt and freshly ground black pepper
2 tsp sunflower oil
1 small onion, peeled and chopped
1 red chilli, deseeded and
  finely chopped
½ tsp ground cumin
½ tsp dried oregano
300 ml/½ pint chicken or
  vegetable stock
1 green pepper, deseeded and sliced
2 tsp cocoa powder
1 tbsp lime juice
2 tsp clear honey
3 tbsp 0%-fat Greek yogurt

To garnish:
sliced limes
red chilli slices
sprig of fresh oregano

To serve:
freshly cooked rice
fresh green salad leaves

1 Using a knife, remove the skin from the chicken joints.

2 In a shallow dish, mix together the flour, paprika, salt and pepper. Coat the chicken on both sides with flour and shake off any excess if necessary.

3 Heat the oil in a large non-stick frying pan. Add the chicken and brown on both sides. Transfer to a plate and reserve.

4 Add the onion and red chilli to the pan and gently cook for 5 minutes, or until the onion is soft. Stir occasionally.

5 Stir in the cumin and oregano and cook for a further minute. Pour in the stock and bring to the boil.

6 Return the chicken to the pan, cover and cook for 40 minutes. Add the green pepper and cook for 10 minutes, until the chicken is cooked. Remove the chicken and pepper with a slotted spoon and keep warm in a serving dish.

7 Blend the cocoa powder with 1 tablespoon of warm water. Stir into the sauce, then boil rapidly until the sauce has thickened and reduced by about one third. Stir in the lime juice, honey and yogurt.

8 Pour the sauce over the chicken and pepper and garnish with the lime slices, chilli and oregano. Serve immediately with the freshly cooked rice and green salad.

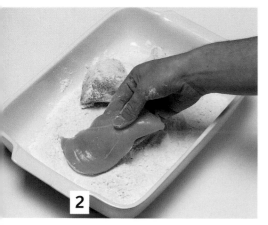
2

5

7

Chicken & New Potatoes on Rosemary Skewers

INGREDIENTS

Serves 4

8 thick fresh rosemary stems,
   at least 23 cm/9 inches long
3–4 tbsp extra virgin olive oil
2 garlic cloves, peeled and crushed
1 tsp freshly chopped thyme
grated rind and juice of 1 lemon
salt and freshly ground black pepper
4 skinless chicken breast fillets
16 small new potatoes, peeled
   or scrubbed
8 very small onions or
   shallots, peeled
1 large yellow or red
   pepper, deseeded
lemon wedges, to garnish
parsley-flavoured cooked rice,
   to serve

1 Preheat the grill and line the grill rack with tinfoil just before cooking. If using a barbecue, light at least 20 minutes before required. Strip the leaves from the rosemary stems, leaving about 5 cm/2 inches of soft leaves at the top. Chop the leaves coarsely and reserve. Using a sharp knife, cut the thicker, woody ends of the stems to a point which can pierce the chicken pieces and potatoes. Blend the chopped rosemary, oil, garlic, thyme and lemon rind and juice in a shallow dish. Season to taste with salt and pepper.

2 Cut the chicken into 4 cm/1½ inch cubes, add to the flavoured oil and stir well. Cover, refrigerate for at least 30 minutes, turning occasionally.

3 Cook the potatoes in lightly salted boiling water for 10–12 minutes until just tender. Add the onions to the potatoes 2 minutes before the end of the cooking time. Drain, rinse under cold running water and leave to cool. Cut the pepper into 2.5 cm/1 inch squares.

4 Beginning with a piece of chicken and starting with the pointed end of the skewer, alternately thread equal amounts of chicken, potato, pepper and onion onto each rosemary skewer. Cover the leafy ends of the skewers with tinfoil to stop them from burning. Do not thread the chicken and vegetables too closely together on the skewer or the chicken may not cook completely.

5 Cook the kebabs for 15 minutes, or until tender and golden, turning and brushing with either extra oil or the marinade. Remove the tinfoil, garnish with lemon wedges and serve on rice.

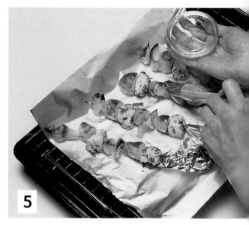

Lemon Chicken with Potatoes, Rosemary & Olives

INGREDIENTS

Serves 6

12 skinless boneless chicken thighs
1 large lemon
125 ml/4 fl oz extra virgin olive oil
6 garlic cloves, peeled and sliced
2 onions, peeled and thinly sliced
bunch of fresh rosemary
1.1 kg/2½ lb potatoes, peeled and cut
   into 4 cm/1½ inch pieces
salt and freshly ground black pepper
18–24 black olives, pitted

To serve:
steamed carrots
courgettes

HELPFUL HINT

It is worth seeking out unwaxed lemons for this recipe, or for any recipe in which the lemon zest is to be eaten. If unwaxed fruit are unavailable, pour hot water over them and scrub well before removing the zest.

1 Preheat oven to 200°C/400°F/Gas Mark 6, 15 minutes before cooking. Trim the chicken thighs and place in a shallow baking dish large enough to hold them in a single layer. Remove the rind from the lemon with a zester or if using a peeler cut into thin julienne strips. Reserve half and add the remainder to the chicken. Squeeze the lemon juice over the chicken, toss to coat well and leave to stand for 10 minutes.

2 Transfer the chicken to a roasting tin. Add the remaining lemon zest or julienne strips, olive oil, garlic, onions and half of the rosemary sprigs. Toss gently and leave for about 20 minutes.

3 Cover the potatoes with lightly salted water and bring to the boil. Cook for 2 minutes, then drain well and add to the chicken. Season to taste with salt and pepper.

4 Roast the chicken in the preheated oven for 50 minutes, turning frequently and basting, or until the chicken is cooked. Just before the end of cooking time, discard the rosemary, and add fresh sprigs of rosemary. Add the olives and stir. Serve immediately with steamed carrots and courgettes.

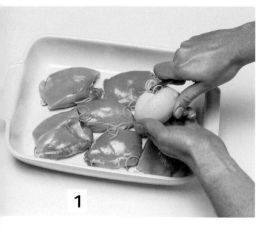
1

2

4

Chicken Parcels with Courgettes & Pasta

INGREDIENTS

Serves 4

2 tbsp olive oil

125 g/4 oz farfalle pasta

1 onion, peeled and thinly sliced

1 garlic clove, peeled and
    finely chopped

2 medium courgettes, trimmed and
    thinly sliced

salt and freshly ground black pepper

2 tbsp freshly chopped oregano

4 plum tomatoes, deseeded and
    coarsely chopped

4 x 175 g/6 oz boneless, skinless
    chicken breasts

150 ml/¼ pint Italian white wine

1 Preheat oven to 200°C/400°F/Gas Mark 6, 15 minutes before cooking. Lightly brush four large sheets of non-stick baking parchment with half the oil. Bring a saucepan of lightly salted water to the boil and cook the pasta for 10 minutes, or until 'al dente'. Drain and reserve.

2 Heat the remaining oil in a frying pan and cook the onion for 2–3 minutes. Add the garlic and cook for 1 minute. Add the courgettes and cook for 1 minute, then remove from the heat, season to taste with salt and pepper and add half the oregano.

3 Divide the cooked pasta equally between the four sheets of baking parchment, positioning the pasta in the centre. Top the pasta with equal amounts of the vegetable mixture, and sprinkle a quarter of the chopped tomatoes over each.

4 Score the surface of each chicken breast about 1 cm/½ inch deep. Place a chicken breast on top of the pasta and sprinkle each with the remaining oregano and the white wine. Fold the edges of the paper along the top, then along each side, creating a sealed envelope.

5 Bake in the preheated oven for 30–35 minutes, or until cooked. Serve immediately.

HELPFUL HINT

This is a great recipe for entertaining. The parcels can be prepared ahead and baked when needed. For a dramatic presentation, serve in the paper.

2

3

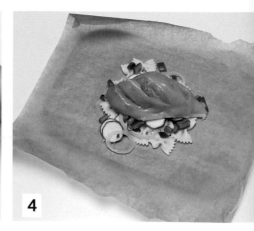

4

Turkey & Oven-roasted Vegetable Salad

INGREDIENTS

Serves 4

6 tbsp olive oil

3 medium courgettes, trimmed
  and sliced

2 yellow peppers, deseeded and sliced

125 g/4 oz pine nuts

275 g/10 oz macaroni

350 g/12 oz cooked turkey

280 g jar or can chargrilled
  artichokes, drained and sliced

225 g/8 oz baby plum
  tomatoes, quartered

4 tbsp freshly chopped coriander

1 garlic clove, peeled and chopped

3 tbsp balsamic vinegar

salt and freshly ground black pepper

HELPFUL HINT

Other vegetables would be equally delicious. Try baby aubergines, trimmed and quartered lengthwise, or scrubbed new potatoes. If you cannot find chargrilled artichokes, use ordinary ones: drain and pat dry, then add to 1 tablespoon of hot olive oil in a frying pan and cook for 2–3 minutes, or until lightly charred.

1 Preheat the oven to 200°C/400°F/Gas Mark 6, 15 minutes before cooking. Line a large roasting tin with tinfoil, pour in half the olive oil and place in the oven for 3 minutes, or until very hot. Remove from the oven, add the courgettes and peppers and stir until evenly coated. Bake for 30–35 minutes, or until slightly charred, turning occasionally.

2 Add the pine nuts to the tin. Return to the oven and bake for 10 minutes, or until the pine nuts are toasted. Remove from the oven and allow the vegetables to cool completely.

3 Bring a large pan of lightly salted water to a rolling boil. Add the macaroni and cook according to the packet instructions, or until 'al dente'. Drain and refresh under cold running water then drain thoroughly and place in a large salad bowl.

4 Cut the turkey into bite-sized pieces and add to the macaroni. Add the artichokes and tomatoes with the cooled vegetables and pan juices to the pan. Blend together the coriander, garlic, remaining oil, vinegar and seasoning. Pour over the salad, toss lightly and serve.

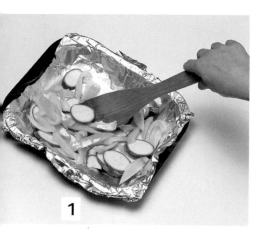

1

2

4

Turkey & Tomato Tagine

INGREDIENTS

Serves 4

For the meatballs:

450 g/1 lb fresh turkey mince
1 small onion, peeled and very
  finely chopped
1 garlic clove, peeled and crushed
1 tbsp freshly chopped coriander
1 tsp ground cumin
1 tbsp olive oil
salt and freshly ground black pepper

For the sauce:

1 onion, peeled and finely chopped
1 garlic clove, peeled and crushed
150 ml/¼ pint turkey stock
400 g can chopped tomatoes
½ tsp ground cumin
½ tsp ground cinnamon
pinch of cayenne pepper
freshly chopped parsley
freshly chopped herbs, to garnish
freshly cooked couscous or rice,
  to serve

1 Preheat the oven to 190°C/375°F/Gas Mark 5. Put all the ingredients for the meatballs in a bowl, except the oil and mix well. Season to taste with salt and pepper. Shape into 20 balls, about the size of walnuts.

2 Put on a tray, cover lightly and chill in the refrigerator while making the sauce.

3 Put the onion and garlic in a pan with 125 ml/4 fl oz of the stock. Cook over a low heat until all the stock has evaporated. Continue cooking for 1 minute, or until the onions begin to colour.

4 Add the remaining stock to the pan with the tomatoes, cumin, cinnamon and cayenne pepper. Simmer for 10 minutes, until slightly thickened and reduced. Stir in the parsley and season to taste.

5 Heat the oil in a large non-stick frying pan and cook the meatballs in two batches until lightly browned all over.

6 Lift the meatballs out with a slotted spoon and drain on kitchen paper.

7 Pour the sauce into a tagine or an ovenproof casserole. Top with the meatballs, cover and cook in the preheated oven for 25–30 minutes, or until the meatballs are cooked through and the sauce is bubbling. Garnish with freshly chopped herbs and serve immediately on a bed of couscous or plain boiled rice.

1

4

6

Turkey Escalopes with Apricot Chutney

INGREDIENTS

Serves 4

4 x 175–225 g/6–8 oz turkey steaks
1 tbsp plain flour
salt and freshly ground black pepper
1 tbsp olive oil
flat-leaf parsley sprigs, to garnish
orange wedges, to serve

For the apricot chutney:

125 g/4 oz no-need-to-soak dried
　apricots, chopped
1 red onion, peeled and
　finely chopped
1 tsp grated fresh root ginger
2 tbsp caster sugar
finely grated rind of ½ orange
125 ml/4 fl oz fresh orange juice
125 ml/4 fl oz ruby port
1 whole clove

1 Put a turkey steak on to a sheet of non-pvc clingfilm or non-stick baking parchment. Cover with a second sheet.

2 Using a rolling pin, gently pound the turkey until the meat is flattened to about 5 mm/¼ inch thick. Repeat to make 4 escalopes.

3 Mix the flour with the salt and pepper and use to lightly dust the turkey escalopes.

4 Put the turkey escalopes on a board or baking tray and cover with a piece of non-pvc clingfilm or non-stick baking parchment. Chill in the refrigerator until ready to cook.

5 For the apricot chutney, put the apricots, onion, ginger, sugar, orange rind, orange juice, port and clove into a saucepan.

6 Slowly bring to the boil and simmer, uncovered for 10 minutes, stirring occasionally, until thick and syrupy.

7 Remove the clove and stir in the chopped coriander.

8 Heat the oil in a pan and chargriddle the turkey escalopes, in two batches if necessary, for 3–4 minutes on each side until golden brown and tender.

9 Spoon the chutney on to four individual serving plates. Place a turkey escalope on top of each spoonful of chutney. Garnish with sprigs of parsley and serve immediately with orange wedges.

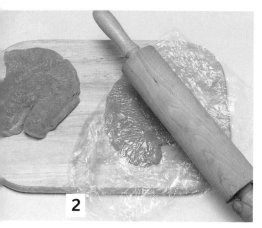

2

5

8

Smoked Turkey Tagliatelle

INGREDIENTS

Serves 4

2 tsp olive oil
1 bunch spring onions, trimmed and diagonally sliced
1 garlic clove, peeled and crushed
1 small courgette, trimmed, sliced and cut in half
4 tbsp dry white wine
400 g can chopped tomatoes
2 tbsp freshly shredded basil
salt and freshly ground black pepper
225 g/8 oz spinach and egg tagliatelle
225 g/8 oz smoked turkey breast, cut into strips
small fresh basil leaves, to garnish

TASTY TIP

Many shops and supermarkets now stock flavoured pasta as well as the plain traditional type. Why not try using a garlic and herb or sundried tomato tagliatelle in this recipe.

1 Heat the oil in a saucepan. Add the spring onions and garlic and gently cook for 2–3 minutes, until beginning to soften. Stir in the sliced courgette and cook for 1 minute.

2 Add the wine and let it bubble for 1–2 minutes. Stir in the chopped tomatoes, bring to the boil and simmer uncovered over a low heat for 15 minutes, or until the courgettes are tender and the sauce slightly reduced. Stir the shredded basil into the sauce and season to taste with salt and pepper.

3 Meanwhile, bring a large pan of salted water to the boil. Add the tagliatelle and cook for 10 minutes, until 'al dente' or according to the packet instructions. Drain thoroughly.

4 Return the tagliatelle to the pan, add half the tomato sauce and toss together to coat the pasta thoroughly in the sauce. Cover with a lid and reserve.

5 Add the strips of turkey to the remaining sauce and heat gently for 2–3 minutes until piping hot.

6 Divide the tagliatelle among four serving plates. Spoon over the sauce, garnish with basil leaves and serve immediately.

Turkey & Mixed Mushroom Lasagne

INGREDIENTS

Serves 4

1 tbsp olive oil

225 g/8 oz mixed mushrooms e.g. button, chestnut and portabello, wiped and sliced

15 g/½ oz butter

25 g/1 oz plain flour

300 ml/½ pint skimmed milk

1 bay leaf

225 g/8 oz cooked turkey, cubed

¼ tsp freshly grated nutmeg

salt and freshly ground black pepper

400 g can plum tomatoes, drained and chopped

1 tsp dried mixed herbs

9 lasagne sheets (about 150 g/5 oz)

For the topping:

200 ml/7 fl oz 0%-fat Greek yogurt

1 medium egg, lightly beaten

1 tbsp finely grated Parmesan cheese

mixed salad leaves, to serve

1 Preheat the oven to 180°C/350°F/Gas 4. Heat the oil and cook the mushrooms until tender and all the juices have evaporated. Remove and reserve.

2 Put the butter, flour, milk and bay leaf in the pan. Slowly bring to the boil, stirring until thickened. Simmer for 2–3 minutes. Remove the bay leaf and stir in the mushrooms, turkey, nutmeg, salt and pepper.

3 Mix together the tomatoes, mixed herbs and season with salt and pepper. Spoon half into the base of a 1.7 litre/3 pint ovenproof dish. Top with 3 sheets of lasagne, then with half the turkey mixture. Repeat the layers, then arrange the remaining 3 sheets of pasta on top.

4 Mix together the yogurt and egg. Spoon over the lasagne, spreading the mixture into the corners. Sprinkle with the Parmesan and bake in the preheated oven for 45 minutes. Serve with the mixed salad.

2

3

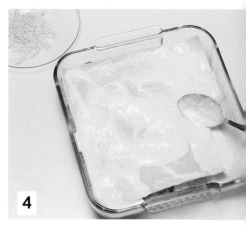

4

Teriyaki Turkey with Oriental Vegetables

INGREDIENTS

Serves 4

1 red chilli

1 garlic clove, peeled and crushed

2.5 cm/1 inch piece root ginger,
    peeled and grated

3 tbsp dark soy sauce

1 tsp sunflower oil

350 g/12 oz skinless, boneless
    turkey breast

1 tbsp sesame oil

1 tbsp sesame seeds

2 carrots, peeled and cut into
    matchstick strips

1 leek, trimmed and shredded

125 g/4 oz broccoli, cut into
    tiny florets

1 tsp cornflour

3 tbsp dry sherry

125 g/4 oz mangetout, cut into
    thin strips

To serve:

freshly cooked egg noodles

sprinkling of sesame seeds

1 Halve, deseed and thinly slice the chilli. Put into a small bowl with the garlic, ginger, soy sauce and sunflower oil.

2 Cut the turkey into thin strips. Add to the mixture and mix until well coated. Cover with clingfilm and marinate in the refrigerator for at least 30 minutes.

3 Heat a wok or large frying pan. Add 2 teaspoons of the sesame oil. When hot, remove the turkey from the marinade. Stir-fry for 2–3 minutes until browned and cooked. Remove from the pan and reserve.

4 Heat the remaining 1 teaspoon of oil in the wok. Add the sesame seeds and stir-fry for a few seconds until they start to change colour.

5 Add the carrots, leek and broccoli and continue stir-frying for 2–3 minutes.

6 Blend the cornflour with 1 tablespoon of cold water to make a smooth paste. Stir in the sherry and marinade. Add to the wok with the mangetout and cook for 1 minute, stirring all the time until thickened.

7 Return the turkey to the pan and continue cooking for 1–2 minutes or until the turkey is hot, the vegetables are tender and the sauce is bubbling. Serve the turkey and vegetables immediately with the egg noodles. Sprinkle with the sesame seeds.

2

3

4

Guinea Fowl with Calvados & Apples

INGREDIENTS

Serves 4

4 guinea fowl supremes, each about
  150 g/5 oz, skinned
1 tbsp plain flour
1 tbsp sunflower oil
1 onion, peeled and finely sliced
1 garlic clove, peeled and crushed
1 tsp freshly chopped thyme
150 ml/¼ pint dry cider
salt and freshly ground black pepper
3 tbsp Calvados brandy
sprigs of fresh thyme, to garnish

For the caramelised apples:

15 g/½ oz unsalted butter
2 red-skinned eating apples,
  quartered, cored and sliced
1 tsp caster sugar

1 Lightly dust the guinea fowl supremes with the flour.

2 Heat 2 teaspoons of the oil in a large non-stick frying pan and cook the supremes for 2–3 minutes on each side until browned. Remove from the pan and reserve.

3 Heat the remaining teaspoon of oil in the pan and add the onion and garlic. Cook over a medium heat for 10 minutes, stirring occasionally until soft and just beginning to colour.

4 Stir in the chopped thyme and cider. Return the guinea fowl to the pan, season with salt and pepper and bring to a very gentle simmer. Cover and cook over a low heat for 15–20 minutes or until the guinea fowl is tender.

5 Remove the guinea fowl and keep warm. Turn up the heat and boil the sauce until thickened and reduced by half.

6 Meanwhile, prepare the caramelised apples. Melt the butter in a small non-stick pan, add the apple slices in a single layer and sprinkle with the sugar. Cook until the apples are tender and beginning to caramelise, turning once.

7 Put the Calvados in a metal ladle or small saucepan and gently heat until warm. Carefully set alight with a match, let the flames die down, then stir into the sauce.

8 Serve the guinea fowl with the sauce spooned over and garnished with the caramelised apples and sprigs of fresh thyme.

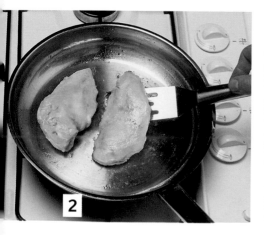

Duck with Berry Sauce

INGREDIENTS

Serves 4

4 x 175 g/6 oz boneless duck breasts
salt and freshly ground black pepper
1 tsp sunflower oil

For the sauce:

juice of 1 orange
1 bay leaf
3 tbsp redcurrant jelly
150 g/5 oz fresh or frozen
  mixed berries
2 tbsp dried cranberries or cherries
½ tsp soft light brown sugar
1 tbsp balsamic vinegar
1 tsp freshly chopped mint
sprigs of fresh mint, to garnish

To serve:

freshly cooked potatoes
freshly cooked green beans

HELPFUL HINT

Duck breasts are best served slightly pink in the middle. Whole ducks, however, should be thoroughly cooked.

1 Remove the skins from the duck breasts and season with a little salt and pepper. Brush a griddle pan with the oil, then heat on the stove until smoking hot.

2 Place the duck, skinned-side down, in the pan. Cook over a medium-high heat for 5 minutes, or until well browned. Turn the duck and cook for 2 minutes. Lower the heat and cook for a further 5–8 minutes, or until cooked, but still slightly pink in the centre. Remove from the pan and keep warm.

3 While the duck is cooking, make the sauce. Put the orange juice, bay leaf, redcurrant jelly, fresh or frozen and dried berries and sugar in a small griddle pan. Add any juices left in the griddle pan to the small pan. Slowly bring to the boil, lower the heat and simmer uncovered for 4–5 minutes, until the fruit is soft.

4 Remove the bay leaf. Stir in the vinegar and chopped mint and season to taste with salt and pepper.

5 Slice the duck breasts on the diagonal and arrange on serving plates. Spoon over the berry sauce and garnish with sprigs of fresh mint. Serve immediately with the potatoes and green beans.

2

3

5

Sticky–glazed Spatchcocked Poussins

INGREDIENTS

Serves 4

2 poussins, each about 700 g/1½ lb
salt and freshly ground black pepper
4 kumquats, thinly sliced
assorted salad leaves, crusty bread
  or new potatoes, to serve

For the glaze:

zest of 1 small lemon, finely grated
1 tbsp lemon juice
1 tbsp dry sherry
2 tbsp clear honey
2 tbsp dark soy sauce
2 tbsp whole-grain mustard
1 tsp tomato purée
½ tsp Chinese five spice powder

1 Preheat the grill just before cooking. Place one of the poussins breast-side down on a board. Using poultry shears, cut down one side of the backbone. Cut down the other side of the backbone. Remove the bone.

2 Open out the poussin and press down hard on the breast bone with the heel of your hand to break it and to flatten the poussin.

3 Thread two skewers crosswise through the bird to keep it flat, ensuring that each skewer goes through a wing and out through the leg on the opposite side. Repeat with the other bird. Season both sides of the bird with salt and pepper.

4 To make the glaze, mix together the lemon zest and juice, sherry, honey, soy sauce, mustard, tomato purée and Chinese five spice powder and use to brush all over the poussins.

5 Place the poussins skin-side down on a grill rack and grill under a medium heat for 15 minutes, brushing halfway through with more glaze.

6 Turn the poussins over and grill for 10 minutes. Brush again with glaze and arrange the kumquat slices on top. Grill for a further 15 minutes until well-browned and cooked through. If they start to brown too quickly, turn down the grill a little.

7 Remove the skewers and cut each poussin in half along the breastbone. Serve immediately with the salad, crusty bread or new potatoes.

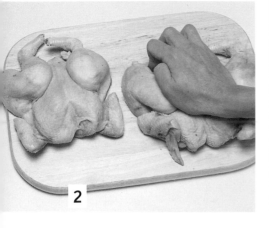

Fillet Steaks with Tomato & Garlic Sauce

INGREDIENTS

Serves 4

700 g/1½ lb ripe tomatoes
2 garlic cloves
2 tbsp olive oil
2 tbsp freshly chopped basil
2 tbsp freshly chopped oregano
2 tbsp red wine
salt and freshly ground black pepper
75 g/3 oz pitted black olives, chopped
4 fillet steaks, about 175 g/6 oz each
  in weight
freshly cooked vegetables, to serve

1 Make a small cross on the top of each tomato and place in a large bowl. Cover with boiling water and leave for 2 minutes. Using a slotted spoon, remove the tomatoes and skin carefully. Repeat until all the tomatoes are skinned. Place on a chopping board, cut into quarters, remove the seeds and roughly chop, then reserve.

2 Peel and chop the garlic. Heat half the olive oil in a saucepan and cook the garlic for 30 seconds. Add the chopped tomatoes with the basil, oregano, red wine and season to taste with salt and pepper. Bring to the boil then reduce the heat, cover and simmer for 15 minutes, stirring occasionally, or until the sauce is reduced and thickened. Stir the olives into the sauce and keep warm while cooking the steaks.

3 Meanwhile, lightly oil a griddle pan or heavy-based frying pan with the remaining olive oil and cook the steaks for 2 minutes on each side to seal. Continue to cook the steaks for a further 2–4 minutes, depending on personal preference. Serve the steaks immediately with the garlic sauce and freshly cooked vegetables.

HELPFUL HINT

Fillet steak should be a deep mahogany colour with a good marbling of fat. If the meat is bright red or if the fat is bright white the meat has not been aged properly and will probably be quite tough.

1

2

3

Italian Beef Pot Roast

INGREDIENTS

Serves 6

1.8 kg/4 lb brisket of beef
225 g/8 oz small onions, peeled
3 garlic cloves, peeled and chopped
2 celery sticks, trimmed and chopped
2 carrots, peeled and sliced
450 g/1 lb ripe tomatoes
300 ml/½ pint Italian red wine
2 tbsp olive oil
300 ml/½ pint beef stock
1 tbsp tomato purée
2 tsp freeze-dried mixed herbs
salt and freshly ground black pepper
25 g/1 oz butter
25 g/1 oz plain flour
freshly cooked vegetables, to serve

HELPFUL HINT

Most supermarkets do not sell brisket, but good butchers will be able to order it. Brisket is an excellent cut for all kinds of pot roasts, but make sure it is professionally trimmed as it can contain a lot of gristle and fat.

1 Preheat oven to 150°C/300°F/Gas Mark 2, 10 minutes before cooking. Place the beef in a bowl. Add the onions, garlic, celery and carrots. Place the tomatoes in a bowl and cover with boiling water. Allow to stand for 2 minutes and drain. Peel away the skins, discard the seeds and chop, then add to the bowl with the red wine. Cover tightly and marinate in the refrigerator overnight.

2 Lift the marinated beef from the bowl and pat dry with absorbent kitchen paper. Heat the olive oil in a large casserole dish and cook the beef until it is browned all over, then remove from the dish. Drain the vegetables from the marinade, reserving the marinade. Add the vegetables to the casserole dish and fry gently for 5 minutes, stirring occasionally, until all the vegetables are browned.

3 Return the beef to the casserole dish with the marinade, beef stock, tomato purée, mixed herbs and season with salt and pepper. Bring to the boil, then cover and cook in the preheated oven for 3 hours.

4 Using a slotted spoon transfer the beef and any large vegetables to a plate and leave in a warm place. Blend the butter and flour to form a paste. Bring the casserole juices to the boil and then gradually stir in small spoonfuls of the paste. Cook until thickened. Serve with the sauce and a selection of vegetables.

Pasta with Beef, Capers & Olives

INGREDIENTS

Serves 4

2 tbsp olive oil

300 g/11 oz rump steak, trimmed and
  cut into strips

4 spring onions, trimmed and sliced

2 garlic cloves, peeled and chopped

2 courgettes, trimmed and cut
  into strips

1 red pepper, deseeded and cut
  into strips

2 tsp freshly chopped oregano

2 tbsp capers, drained and rinsed

4 tbsp pitted black olives, sliced

400 g can chopped tomatoes

salt and freshly ground black pepper

450 g/1 lb fettuccine

1 tbsp freshly chopped parsley,
  to garnish

TASTY TIP

When cooking the beef, it is important that it fries rather than steams in the pan, giving a beautifully brown and caramelised outside while keeping the middle moist and tender. Make sure that the oil in the pan is hot so that the strips of beef sizzle when added.

1 Heat the olive oil in a large frying pan over a high heat. Add the steak and cook, stirring, for 3–4 minutes, or until browned. Remove from the pan using a slotted spoon and reserve.

2 Lower the heat, add the spring onions and garlic to the pan and cook for 1 minute. Add the courgettes and pepper and cook for 3–4 minutes.

3 Add the oregano, capers and olives to the pan with the chopped tomatoes. Season to taste with salt and pepper, then simmer for 7 minutes, stirring occasionally. Return the beef to the pan and simmer for 3–5 minutes, or until the sauce has thickened slightly.

4 Meanwhile, bring a large pan of lightly salted water to a rolling boil. Add the pasta and cook according to the packet instructions, or until 'al dente'.

5 Drain the pasta thoroughly. Return to the pan and add the beef sauce. Toss gently until the pasta is lightly coated. Tip into a warmed serving dish or on to individual plates. Sprinkle with chopped parsley and serve immediately.

Tagliatelle with Broccoli & Sesame

INGREDIENTS

Serves 2

225 g/8 oz broccoli, cut into florets
125 g/4 oz baby corn
175 g/6 oz dried tagliatelle
1½ tbsp tahini paste
1 tbsp dark soy sauce
1 tbsp dark muscovado sugar
1 tbsp red wine vinegar
1 tbsp sunflower oil
1 garlic clove, peeled and
    finely chopped
2.5 cm/1 inch piece fresh root ginger,
    peeled and shredded
½ tsp dried chilli flakes
salt and freshly ground black pepper
1 tbsp toasted sesame seeds
slices of radish, to garnish

1 Bring a large saucepan of salted water to the boil and add the broccoli and corn. Return the water to the boil then remove the vegetables at once using a slotted spoon, reserving the water. Plunge them into cold water and drain well. Dry on kitchen paper and reserve.

2 Return the water to the boil. Add the tagliatelle and cook until 'al dente' or according to the packet instructions. Drain well. Run under cold water until cold, then drain well again.

3 Place the tahini, soy sauce, sugar and vinegar into a bowl. Mix well, then reserve. Heat the oil in a wok or large frying pan over a high heat and add the garlic, ginger and chilli flakes and stir-fry for about 30 seconds. Add the broccoli and baby corn and continue to stir-fry for about 3 minutes.

4 Add the tagliatelle to the wok along with the tahini mixture and stir together for a further 1–2 minutes until heated through. Season to taste with salt and pepper. Sprinkle with sesame seeds, garnish with the radish slices and serve immediately.

FOOD FACT

Tahini is made from ground sesame seeds and is generally available in large supermarkets and Middle Eastern shops. It is most often used in hummus.

1

3

4

Pasta with Courgettes, Rosemary & Lemon

INGREDIENTS

Serves 4

350 g/12 oz dried pasta shapes,
　e.g. rigatoni
1½ tbsp good quality extra virgin
　olive oil
2 garlic cloves, peeled and
　finely chopped
4 medium courgettes, thinly sliced
1 tbsp freshly chopped rosemary
1 tbsp freshly chopped parsley
zest and juice of 2 lemons
25 g/1 oz pitted black olives,
　roughly chopped
25 g/1 oz pitted green olives,
　roughly chopped
salt and freshly ground black pepper

To garnish:
lemon slices
sprigs of fresh rosemary

1 Bring a large saucepan of salted water to the boil and add the pasta.

2 Return to the boil and cook until 'al dente' or according to the packet instructions.

3 Meanwhile, when the pasta is almost done, heat the oil in a large frying pan and add the garlic.

4 Cook over a medium heat until the garlic just begins to brown. Be careful not to overcook the garlic at this stage or it will become bitter.

5 Add the courgettes, rosemary, parsley and lemon zest and juice. Cook for 3–4 minutes until the courgettes are just tender.

6 Add the olives to the frying pan and stir well. Season to taste with salt and pepper and remove from the heat.

7 Drain the pasta well and add to the frying pan. Stir until thoroughly combined. Garnish with lemon and sprigs of fresh rosemary and serve immediately.

4

5

7

Spring Vegetable & Herb Risotto

INGREDIENTS

Serves 2-3

1 litre/1¾ pint vegetable stock

125 g/4 oz asparagus tips, trimmed

125 g/4 oz baby carrots, scrubbed

50 g/2 oz peas, fresh or frozen

50 g/2 oz fine French beans, trimmed

1 tbsp olive oil

1 onion, peeled and finely chopped

1 garlic clove, peeled and
   finely chopped

2 tsp freshly chopped thyme

225 g/8 oz risotto rice

150 ml/¼ pint white wine

1 tbsp each freshly chopped basil,
   chives and parsley

zest of ½ lemon

3 tbsp half-fat crème fraîche

salt and freshly ground black pepper

1   Bring the vegetable stock to the boil in a large saucepan and add the asparagus, baby carrots, peas and beans. Bring the stock back to the boil and remove the vegetables at once using a slotted spoon. Rinse under cold running water. Drain again and reserve. Keep the stock hot.

2   Heat the oil in a large deep frying pan and add the onion. Cook over a medium heat for 4–5 minutes until starting to brown. Add the garlic and thyme and cook for a further few seconds. Add the rice and stir well for a minute until the rice is hot and coated in oil.

3   Add the white wine and stir constantly until the wine is almost completely absorbed by the rice. Begin adding the stock a ladleful at a time, stirring well and waiting until the last ladleful has been absorbed before stirring in the next. Add the vegetables after using about half of the stock. Continue until all the stock is used. This will take 20–25 minutes. The rice and vegetables should both be tender.

4   Remove the pan from the heat. Stir in the herbs, lemon zest and crème fraîche. Season to taste with salt and pepper and serve immediately.

FOOD FACT

In Italy, they use different types of rice, such as Arborio and Carnaroli, depending on whether the risotto is vegetable, meat or fish-based.

Baby Onion Risotto

INGREDIENTS

Serves 4

For the baby onions:

1 tbsp olive oil

450 g/1 lb baby onions, peeled
   and halved if large

pinch of sugar

1 tbsp freshly chopped thyme

For the risotto:

1 tbsp olive oil

1 small onion, peeled and
   finely chopped

2 garlic cloves, peeled and
   finely chopped

350 g/12 oz risotto rice

150 ml/¹⁄₄ pint red wine

1 litre/1³⁄₄ pint hot vegetable stock

125 g/4 oz low-fat soft goat's cheese

salt and freshly ground black pepper

sprigs of fresh thyme, to garnish

rocket leaves, to serve

FOOD FACT

To peel baby onions, put into a saucepan of water and bring to the boil. Drain and run under cold water. The skins will loosen and peel easily.

1 For the baby onions, heat the olive oil in a saucepan and add the onions with the sugar. Cover and cook over a low heat, stirring occasionally, for 20–25 minutes until caramelised. Uncover during the last 10 minutes of cooking.

2 Meanwhile, for the risotto, heat the oil in a large frying pan and add the onion. Cook over a medium heat for 5 minutes until softened. Add the garlic and cook for a further 30 seconds.

3 Add the risotto rice and stir well. Add the red wine and stir constantly until the wine is almost completely absorbed by the rice. Begin adding the stock a ladleful at a time, stirring well and waiting until the last ladleful has been absorbed before stirring in the next. It will take 20–25 minutes to add all the stock by which time the rice should be just cooked but still firm. Remove from the heat.

4 Add the thyme to the onions and cook briefly. Increase the heat and allow the onion mixture to bubble for 2–3 minutes until almost evaporated. Add the onion mixture to the risotto along with the goat's cheese. Stir well and season to taste with salt and pepper. Garnish with sprigs of fresh thyme. Serve immediately with the rocket leaves.

Brown Rice Spiced Pilaf

INGREDIENTS

Serves 4

1 tbsp vegetable oil

1 tbsp blanched almonds, flaked
   or chopped

1 onion, peeled and chopped

1 carrot, peeled and diced

225 g/8 oz flat mushrooms,
   sliced thickly

¼ tsp cinnamon

large pinch dried chilli flakes

50 g/2 oz dried apricots,
   roughly chopped

25 g/1 oz currants

zest of 1 orange

350 g/12 oz brown basmati rice

900 ml/1½ pints vegetable stock

2 tbsp freshly chopped coriander

2 tbsp freshly snipped chives

salt and freshly ground black pepper

snipped chives, to garnish

1 Preheat the oven to 200°C/400°F/Gas Mark 6. Heat the oil in a large flameproof casserole and add the almonds. Cook for 1–2 minutes until just browning. (Be very careful as the nuts will burn very easily).

2 Add the onion and carrot. Cook for 5 minutes until softened and starting to turn brown. Add the mushrooms and cook for a further 5 minutes, stirring often.

3 Add the cinnamon and chilli flakes and cook for about 30 seconds before adding the apricots, currants, orange zest and rice.

4 Stir together well and add the stock. Bring to the boil, cover tightly and transfer to the preheated oven. Cook for 45 minutes until the rice and vegetables are tender.

5 Stir the coriander and chives into the pilaf and season to taste with salt and pepper. Garnish with the extra chives and serve immediately.

2

3

5

Spiced Couscous & Vegetables

INGREDIENTS

Serves 4

1 tbsp olive oil

1 large shallot, peeled and
  finely chopped

1 garlic clove, peeled and
  finely chopped

1 small red pepper, deseeded and cut
  into strips

1 small yellow pepper, deseeded and
  cut into strips

1 small aubergine, diced

1 tsp each turmeric, ground cumin,
  ground cinnamon and paprika

2 tsp ground coriander

large pinch saffron strands

2 tomatoes, peeled, deseeded
  and diced

2 tbsp lemon juice

225 g/8 oz couscous

225 ml/8 fl oz vegetable stock

2 tbsp raisins

2 tbsp whole almonds

2 tbsp freshly chopped parsley

2 tbsp freshly chopped coriander

salt and freshly ground black pepper

1 Heat the oil in a large frying pan and add the shallot and garlic and cook for 2–3 minutes until softened. Add the peppers and aubergine and reduce the heat.

2 Cook for 8–10 minutes until the vegetables are tender, adding a little water if necessary.

3 Test a piece of aubergine to ensure it is cooked through. Add all the spices and cook for a further minute, stirring.

4 Increase the heat and add the tomatoes and lemon juice. Cook for 2–3 minutes until the tomatoes have started to break down. Remove from the heat and leave to cool slightly.

5 Meanwhile, put the couscous into a large bowl. Bring the stock to the boil in a saucepan, then pour over the couscous. Stir well and cover with a clean tea towel.

6 Leave to stand for 7–8 minutes until all the stock is absorbed and the couscous is tender.

7 Uncover the couscous and fluff with a fork. Stir in the vegetable and spice mixture along with the raisins, almonds, parsley and coriander. Season to taste with salt and pepper and serve.

3

5

7

Black Bean Chilli with Avocado Salsa

INGREDIENTS

Serves 4

250 g/9 oz black beans and black-eye
  beans, soaked overnight

2 tbsp olive oil

1 large onion, peeled and
  finely chopped

1 red pepper, deseeded and diced

2 garlic cloves, peeled and
  finely chopped

1 red chilli, deseeded and
  finely chopped

2 tsp chilli powder

1 tsp ground cumin

2 tsp ground coriander

400 g can chopped tomatoes

450 ml/¾ pint vegetable stock

1 small ripe avocado, diced

½ small red onion, peeled and
  finely chopped

2 tbsp freshly chopped coriander

juice of 1 lime

1 small tomato, peeled, deseeded
  and diced

salt and freshly ground black pepper

25 g/1 oz dark chocolate

To garnish:

half-fat crème fraîche

lime slices

sprigs of coriander

1 Drain the beans and place in a large saucepan with at least twice their volume of fresh water.

2 Bring slowly to the boil, skimming off any froth that rises to the surface. Boil rapidly for 10 minutes, then reduce the heat and simmer for about 45 minutes, adding more water if necessary. Drain and reserve.

3 Heat the oil in a large saucepan and add the onion and pepper. Cook for 3–4 minutes until softened. Add the garlic and chilli. Cook for 5 minutes, or until the onion and pepper have softened. Add the chilli powder, cumin and coriander and cook for 30 seconds. Add the beans along with the tomatoes and stock.

4 Bring to the boil and simmer uncovered for 40–45 minutes until the beans and vegetables are tender and the sauce has reduced.

5 Mix together the avocado, onion, fresh coriander, lime juice and tomato. Season with salt and pepper and set aside. Remove the chilli from the heat. Break the chocolate into pieces. Sprinkle over the chilli. Leave for 2 minutes. Stir well. Garnish with crème fraîche, lime and coriander. Serve with the avocado salsa.

Boston–style Baked Beans

INGREDIENTS

Serves 8

350 g/12 oz mixed dried pulses, e.g.
  haricot, flageolet, cannellini,
  chickpeas or pinto beans
1 large onion, peeled and
  finely chopped
125 g/4 oz black treacle or molasses
2 tbsp Dijon mustard
2 tbsp light brown soft sugar
125 g/4 oz plain flour
150 g/5 oz fine cornmeal
2 tbsp caster sugar
2½ tsp baking powder
½ tsp salt
2 tbsp freshly chopped thyme
2 medium eggs
200 ml/7 fl oz milk
2 tbsp melted butter
salt and freshly ground black pepper
parsley sprigs, to garnish

1 Preheat the oven to 130°C/250°F/Gas Mark ½. Put the pulses into a large saucepan and cover with at least twice their volume of water. Bring to the boil and simmer for 2 minutes. Leave to stand for 1 hour. Return to the boil and boil rapidly for about 10 minutes. Drain and reserve.

2 Mix together the onion, treacle or molasses, mustard and sugar in a large mixing bowl. Add the drained beans and 300 ml/½ pint fresh water. Stir well, bring to the boil, cover and transfer to the preheated oven for 4 hours in an ovenproof dish, stirring once every hour and adding more water if necessary.

3 When the beans are cooked, remove from the oven and keep warm. Increase the oven temperature to 200°C/400°F/Gas Mark 6. Mix together the plain flour, cornmeal, caster sugar, baking powder, salt and most of the thyme, reserving about one third for garnish. In a separate bowl beat the eggs, then stir in the milk and butter. Pour the wet ingredients on to the dry ones and stir just enough to combine.

4 Pour into a buttered 18 cm/7 inch square cake tin. Sprinkle over the remaining thyme. Bake for 30 minutes until golden and risen or until a toothpick inserted into the centre comes out clean. Cut into squares, then reheat the beans. Season to taste with salt and pepper and serve immediately, garnished with parsley sprigs.

TASTY TIP

For non-vegetarians, add 125 g/4 oz cooked salt pork to the beans as a tasty alternative.

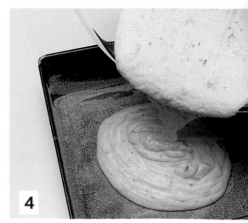

Pumpkin & Chickpea Curry

INGREDIENTS

Serves 4

1 tbsp vegetable oil
1 small onion, peeled and sliced
2 garlic cloves, peeled and
  finely chopped
2.5 cm/1 inch piece root ginger,
  peeled and grated
1 tsp ground coriander
½ tsp ground cumin
½ tsp ground turmeric
¼ tsp ground cinnamon
2 tomatoes, chopped
2 red bird's eye chillies, deseeded
  and finely chopped
450 g/1 lb pumpkin or butternut
  squash flesh, cubed
1 tbsp hot curry paste
300 ml/½ pint vegetable stock
1 large firm banana
400 g can chickpeas, drained
  and rinsed
salt and freshly ground black pepper
1 tbsp freshly chopped coriander
coriander sprigs, to garnish
rice or naan bread, to serve

1 Heat 1 tablespoon of the oil in a saucepan and add the onion. Fry gently for 5 minutes until softened.

2 Add the garlic, ginger and spices and fry for a further minute. Add the chopped tomatoes and chillies and cook for another minute.

3 Add the pumpkin and curry paste and fry gently for 3–4 minutes before adding the stock.

4 Stir well, bring to the boil and simmer for 20 minutes until the pumpkin is tender.

5 Thickly slice the banana and add to the pumpkin along with the chickpeas. Simmer for a further 5 minutes.

6 Season to taste with salt and pepper and add the chopped coriander. Serve immediately, garnished with coriander sprigs and some rice or naan bread.

Roasted Butternut Squash

INGREDIENTS

Serves 4

2 small butternut squash
4 garlic cloves, peeled and crushed
1 tbsp olive oil
salt and freshly ground black pepper
1 tbsp walnut oil
4 medium-sized leeks, trimmed,
  cleaned and thinly sliced
1 tbsp black mustard seeds
300 g can cannellini beans, drained
  and rinsed
125 g/4 oz fine French beans, halved
150 ml/¼ pint vegetable stock
50 g/2 oz rocket
2 tbsp freshly snipped chives
fresh chives, to garnish

To serve:

4 tbsp low-fat fromage frais
mixed salad

1 Preheat the oven to 200°C/400°F/Gas Mark 6. Cut the butternut squash in half lengthwise and scoop out all of the seeds.

2 Score the squash in a diamond pattern with a sharp knife. Mix the garlic with the olive oil and brush over the cut surfaces of the squash. Season well with salt and pepper. Put on a baking sheet and roast for 40 minutes until tender.

3 Heat the walnut oil in a saucepan and fry the leeks and mustard seeds for 5 minutes.

4 Add the drained cannellini beans, French beans and vegetable stock. Bring to the boil and simmer gently for 5 minutes until the French beans are tender.

5 Remove from the heat and stir in the rocket and chives. Season well. Remove the squash from the oven and allow to cool for 5 minutes. Spoon in the bean mixture. Garnish with a few snipped chives and serve immediately with the fromage frais and a mixed salad.

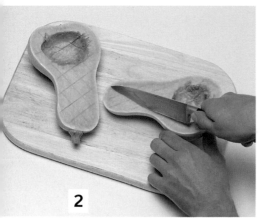

2

3

5

Vegetable Cassoulet

INGREDIENTS

Serves 6

125 g/4 oz dried haricot beans,
  soaked overnight
2 tbsp olive oil
2 garlic cloves, peeled and chopped
225 g/8 oz baby onions, peeled
  and halved
2 carrots, peeled and diced
2 celery sticks, trimmed and
  finely chopped
1 red pepper, deseeded and chopped
175 g/6 oz mixed mushrooms, sliced
1 tbsp each freshly chopped
  rosemary, thyme and sage
150 ml/¼ pint red wine
4 tbsp tomato purée
1 tbsp dark soy sauce
salt and freshly ground black pepper
50 g/2 oz fresh breadcrumbs
1 tbsp freshly chopped parsley
basil sprigs, to garnish

1   Preheat the oven to 190°C/375°F/Gas Mark 5. Drain the haricot beans and place in a saucepan with 1.1 litres/2 pints of fresh water. Bring to the boil and boil rapidly for 10 minutes. Reduce the heat and simmer gently for 45 minutes. Drain the beans, reserving 300 ml/½ pint of the liquid.

2   Heat 1 tablespoon of the oil in a flameproof casserole and add the garlic, onions, carrot, celery and red pepper. Cook gently for 10–12 minutes until tender and starting to brown. Add a little water if the vegetables start to stick. Add the mushrooms and cook for a further 5 minutes until softened. Add the herbs and stir briefly.

3   Stir in the red wine and boil rapidly for about 5 minutes until reduced and syrupy. Stir in the reserved beans and their liquid, tomato purée and soy sauce. Season to taste with salt and pepper.

4   Mix together the breadcrumbs and parsley with the remaining 1 tablespoon of oil. Scatter this mixture evenly over the top of the stew. Cover loosely with foil and transfer to the preheated oven. Cook for 30 minutes. Carefully remove the foil and cook for a further 15–20 minutes until the topping is crisp and golden. Serve immediately, garnished with basil sprigs.

HELPFUL HINT

If cooking dried haricot beans is too time-consuming, then substitute with canned beans instead.

Creamy Puy Lentils

INGREDIENTS

Serves 4

225 g/8 oz puy lentils
1 tbsp olive oil
1 garlic clove, peeled and
 finely chopped
zest and juice of 1 lemon
1 tsp whole-grain mustard
1 tbsp freshly chopped tarragon
3 tbsp half-fat crème fraîche
salt and freshly ground black pepper
2 small tomatoes, deseeded
 and chopped
50 g/2 oz pitted black olives
1 tbsp freshly chopped parsley

To garnish:

sprigs of fresh tarragon
lemon wedges

FOOD FACT

Puy lentils are smaller and fatter than green lentils and have a pretty mottled colouring, ranging from gold through to green. They keep their shape and firm texture when cooked.

1 Put the lentils in a saucepan with plenty of cold water and bring to the boil.

2 Boil rapidly for 10 minutes, reduce the heat and simmer gently for a further 20 minutes until just tender. Drain well.

3 Meanwhile, prepare the dressing. Heat the oil in a frying pan over a medium heat.

4 Add the garlic and cook for about a minute until just beginning to brown. Add the lemon zest and juice.

5 Add the mustard and cook for a further 30 seconds.

6 Add the tarragon and crème fraîche and season to taste with salt and pepper.

7 Simmer and add the drained lentils, tomatoes and olives.

8 Transfer to a serving dish and sprinkle the chopped parsley on top.

9 Garnish the lentils with the tarragon sprigs and the lemon wedges and serve immediately.

Panzanella

INGREDIENTS

Serves 4

250 g/9 oz day-old Italian-style bread
1 tbsp red wine vinegar
4 tbsp olive oil
1 tsp lemon juice
1 small garlic clove, peeled and
  finely chopped
1 red onion, peeled and finely sliced
1 cucumber, peeled if preferred
225 g/8 oz ripe tomatoes, deseeded
150 g/5 oz pitted black olives
about 20 basil leaves, coarsely torn or
  left whole if small
sea salt and freshly ground
  black pepper

TASTY TIP

Choose an open-textured Italian-style bread such as ciabatta for this classic Tuscany salad. Look in your local delicatessen for different flavoured marinated olives. Try chilli and garlic, or basil, garlic and orange.

1 Cut the bread into thick slices, leaving the crusts on. Add 1 teaspoon of red wine vinegar to a jug of iced water, put the slices of bread in a bowl and pour over the water. Make sure the bread is covered completely. Leave to soak for 3–4 minutes until just soft.

2 Remove the soaked bread from the water and squeeze it gently, first with your hands and then in a clean tea towel to remove any excess water. Put the bread on a plate, cover with clingfilm and chill in the refrigerator for about 1 hour.

3 Meanwhile, whisk together the olive oil, the remaining red wine vinegar and lemon juice in a large serving bowl. Add the garlic and onion and stir to coat well.

4 Halve the cucumber and remove the seeds. Chop both the cucumber and tomatoes into 1 cm/½ inch dice. Add to the garlic and onions with the olives. Tear the bread into bite-sized chunks and add to the bowl with the fresh basil leaves. Toss together to mix and serve immediately, with a grinding of sea salt and black pepper.

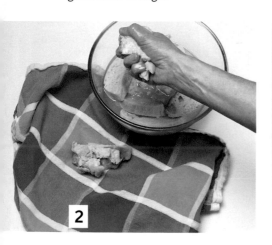

2

3

4

Venetian–style Vegetables & Beans

INGREDIENTS

Serves 4

250 g/9 oz dried pinto beans
3 sprigs of fresh parsley
1 sprig of fresh rosemary
2 tbsp olive oil
200 g can chopped tomatoes
2 shallots, peeled

For the vegetable mixture:

1 large red onion, peeled
1 large white onion, peeled
1 medium carrot, peeled
2 sticks celery, trimmed
3 tbsp olive oil
3 bay leaves
1 tsp caster sugar
3 tbsp red wine vinegar
salt and freshly ground black pepper

HELPFUL HINT

If time is short, put the beans into a large saucepan and cover with cold water. Bring to the boil and boil rapidly for 10 minutes. Turn off the heat and leave to stand for 2 hours. Drain well and cover with fresh water. Cook as above.

1   Put the beans in a bowl, cover with plenty of cold water and leave to soak for at least 8 hours, or overnight.

2   Drain and rinse the beans. Put in a large saucepan with 1.1 litres/ 2 pints cold water. Tie the parsley and rosemary in muslin and add to the beans with the olive oil. Boil rapidly for 10 minutes, then lower the heat and simmer for 20 minutes with the saucepan half-covered. Stir in the tomatoes and shallots and simmer for a further 10–15 minutes, or until the beans are cooked.

3   Meanwhile, slice the red and white onion into rings and then finely dice the carrot and celery. Heat the olive oil in a saucepan and cook the onions over a very low heat for about 10 minutes. Add the carrot, celery and bay leaves to the saucepan and cook for a further 10 minutes, stirring frequently, until the vegetables are tender. Sprinkle with sugar, stir and cook for 1 minute.

4   Stir in the vinegar. Cook for 1 minute, then remove the saucepan from the heat. Drain the beans through a fine sieve, discarding all the herbs, then add the beans to the onion mixture and season well with salt and pepper. Mix gently, then tip the beans into a large serving bowl. Leave to cool, then serve at room temperature.

Peperonata

INGREDIENTS

Serves 6

2 red peppers
2 yellow peppers
450 g/1 lb waxy potatoes
1 large onion
2 tbsp good quality virgin olive oil
700 g/1½ lb tomatoes, peeled,
  deseeded and chopped
2 small courgettes
50 g/2 oz pitted black olives, quartered
small handful basil leaves
salt and freshly ground black pepper
crusty bread, to serve

FOOD FACT

This dish is delicious served with Parmesan melba toasts. To make, simply remove the crusts from 4 slices of thin white bread. Lightly toast and allow to cool before splitting each piece in half by slicing horizontally. Cut diagonally into triangles, place under a hot grill and toast each side for a few minutes until golden and curling at the edges. Sprinkle with finely grated fresh Parmesan cheese and melt under the grill.

1 Prepare the peppers by halving them lengthwise and removing the stems, seeds, and membranes.

2 Cut the peppers lengthwise into strips about 1 cm/½ inch wide. Peel the potatoes and cut into rough dice, about 2.5–3 cm/1–1¼ inch across. Cut the onion lengthwise into 8 wedges.

3 Heat the olive oil in a large saucepan over a medium heat.

4 Add the onion and cook for about 5 minutes, or until starting to brown.

5 Add the peppers, potatoes, tomatoes, courgettes, black olives and about 4 torn basil leaves. Season to taste with salt and pepper.

6 Stir the mixture, cover and cook over a very low heat for about 40 minutes, or until the vegetables are tender but still hold their shape. Garnish with the remaining basil. Transfer to a serving bowl and serve immediately, with chunks of crusty bread.

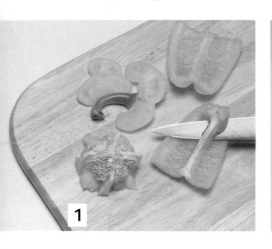

1

4

5

Mushroom Stew

INGREDIENTS

Serves 4

15 g/½ oz dried porcini mushrooms
900 g/2 lb assorted fresh
   mushrooms, wiped
2 tbsp good quality virgin olive oil
1 onion, peeled and finely chopped
2 garlic cloves, peeled and
   finely chopped
1 tbsp fresh thyme leaves
pinch of ground cloves
salt and freshly ground black pepper
700 g/1½ lb tomatoes, peeled,
   deseeded and chopped
225 g/8 oz instant polenta
600ml/1 pint vegetable stock
3 tbsp freshly chopped mixed herbs
sprigs of parsley, to garnish

TASTY TIP

For a dinner party version of this recipe, add a generous splash of vegetarian red wine with the soaking liquid in step 5 and just before serving, remove from the heat and stir in 2 tablespoons of low-fat Greek yogurt.

1 Soak the porcini mushrooms in a small bowl of hot water for 20 minutes.

2 Drain reserving the porcini mushrooms and their soaking liquor. Cut the fresh mushrooms in half and reserve.

3 In a saucepan, heat the oil and add the onion.

4 Cook gently for 5–7 minutes until softened. Add the garlic, thyme and cloves and continue cooking for 2 minutes.

5 Add all the mushrooms and cook for 8–10 minutes until the mushrooms have softened, stirring often. Season to taste with salt and pepper and add the tomatoes and the reserved soaking liquid.

6 Simmer, partly-covered, over a low heat for about 20 minutes until thickened. Adjust the seasoning to taste.

7 Meanwhile, cook the polenta according to the packet instructions using the vegetable stock. Stir in the herbs and divide between four dishes.

8 Ladle the mushrooms over the polenta, garnish with the parsley and serve immediately.

5

6

7

Bulghur Wheat Salad with Minty Lemon Dressing

INGREDIENTS

Serves 2

125 g/4 oz bulghur wheat
10 cm /4 inch piece cucumber
2 shallots, peeled
125 g/4 oz baby sweetcorn
3 ripe but firm tomatoes

Dressing:

grated rind of 1 lemon
3 tbsp lemon juice
3 tbsp freshly chopped mint
2 tbsp freshly chopped parsley
1–2 tsp clear honey
2 tbsp sunflower oil
salt and freshly ground
  black pepper

FOOD FACT

This dish is loosely based on the Middle Eastern dish tabbouleh, a type of salad in which all the ingredients are mixed together and served cold.

1 Place the bulghur wheat in a saucepan and cover with boiling water.

2 Simmer for about 10 minutes, then drain thoroughly and turn into a serving bowl.

3 Cut the cucumber into small dice, chop the shallots finely and reserve. Steam the sweetcorn over a pan of boiling water for 10 minutes or until tender. Drain and slice into thick chunks.

4 Cut a cross on the top of each tomato and place in boiling water until their skins start to peel away.

5 Remove the skins and the seeds and cut the tomatoes into small dice.

6 Make the dressing by briskly whisking all the ingredients in a small bowl until mixed well.

7 When the bulghur wheat has cooled a little, add all the prepared vegetables and stir in the dressing. Season to taste with salt and pepper and serve.

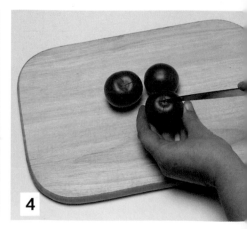

Chinese Salad with Soy & Ginger Dressing

INGREDIENTS

Serves 4

1 head of Chinese cabbage
200 g can water chestnuts, drained
6 spring onions, trimmed
4 ripe but firm cherry tomatoes
125 g/4 oz mangetout
125 g/4 oz beansprouts
2 tbsp freshly chopped coriander

For the soy and ginger dressing:

2 tbsp sunflower oil
4 tbsp light soy sauce
2.5 cm/1 inch piece root ginger,
   peeled and finely grated
zest and juice of 1 lemon
salt and freshly ground black pepper
crusty white bread, to serve

TASTY TIP

Cut 2 skinless chicken breasts into strips, marinate in 2 tablespoons of light soy sauce, 1 tablespoon of oil and 1 finely chopped clove of garlic. Stir-fry. Serve on top of the salad with some sesame seeds.

1 Rinse and finely shred the Chinese cabbage and place in a serving dish.

2 Slice the water chestnuts into small slivers and cut the spring onions diagonally into 2.5 cm/1 inch lengths, then split lengthwise into thin strips.

3 Cut the tomatoes in half and then slice each half into 3 wedges and reserve.

4 Simmer the mangetout in boiling water for 2 minutes until beginning to soften, drain and cut in half diagonally.

5 Arrange the water chestnuts, spring onions, mangetout, tomatoes and beansprouts on top of the shredded Chinese cabbage. Garnish with the freshly chopped coriander.

6 Make the dressing by whisking all the ingredients together in a small bowl until mixed thoroughly. Serve with the bread and the salad.

2

3

4

Curly Endive & Seafood Salad

INGREDIENTS

Serves 4

1 head of curly endive lettuce
2 green peppers
12.5 cm/5 inch piece cucumber
125 g/4 oz squid, cleaned and cut into
  thin rings
225 g/8 oz baby asparagus spears
125 g/4 oz smoked salmon slices,
  cut into wide strips
175 g/6 oz fresh cooked mussels
  in their shells

For the lemon dressing:

2 tbsp sunflower oil
1 tbsp white wine vinegar
5 tbsp fresh lemon juice
1–2 tsp caster sugar
1 tsp mild whole-grain mustard
salt and freshly ground black pepper

To garnish:

slices of lemon
sprigs of fresh coriander

1 Rinse and tear the endive into small pieces and arrange on a serving platter.

2 Remove the seeds from the peppers and cut the peppers and the cucumber into small dice. Sprinkle over the endive.

3 Bring a saucepan of water to the boil and add the squid rings. Bring the pan up to the boil again, then switch off the heat and leave it to stand for 5 minutes. Then drain and rinse thoroughly in cold water.

4 Cook the asparagus in boiling water for 5 minutes or until tender but just crisp. Arrange with the squid, smoked salmon and mussels on top of the salad.

5 To make the lemon dressing, put all the ingredients into a screw-topped jar or into a small bowl and mix thoroughly until the ingredients are combined.

6 Spoon 3 tablespoons of the dressing over the salad and serve the remainder in a small jug. Garnish the salad with slices of lemon and sprigs of coriander and serve.

2

3

4

Marinated Vegetable Kebabs

INGREDIENTS

Serves 4

2 small courgettes, cut into
  2 cm/³/₄ inch pieces
¹/₂ green pepper, deseeded and cut
  into 2.5 cm/1 inch pieces
¹/₂ red pepper, deseeded and cut into
  2.5 cm/1 inch pieces
¹/₂ yellow pepper, deseeded and cut
  into 2.5 cm/1 inch pieces
8 baby onions, peeled
8 button mushrooms
8 cherry tomatoes
freshly chopped parsley, to garnish
freshly cooked couscous, to serve

For the marinade:

1 tbsp light olive oil
4 tbsp dry sherry
2 tbsp light soy sauce
1 red chilli, deseeded and
  finely chopped
2 garlic cloves, peeled and crushed
2.5 cm/1 inch piece root ginger,
  peeled and finely grated

1 Place the courgettes, peppers and baby onions in a pan of just boiled water. Bring back to the boil and simmer for about 30 seconds.

2 Drain and rinse the cooked vegetables in cold water and dry on absorbent kitchen paper.

3 Thread the cooked vegetables and the mushrooms and tomatoes alternately on to skewers and place in a large shallow dish.

4 Make the marinade by whisking all the ingredients together until thoroughly blended. Pour the marinade evenly over the kebabs, then chill in the refrigerator for at least 1 hour. Spoon the marinade over the kebabs occasionally during this time.

5 Place the kebabs in a hot griddle pan or on a hot barbecue and cook gently for 10–12 minutes. Turn the kebabs frequently and brush with the marinade when needed. When the vegetables are tender, sprinkle over the chopped parsley and serve immediately with couscous.

3

4

5

Spanish Baked Tomatoes

INGREDIENTS

Serves 4

175 g/6 oz whole-grain rice
600 ml/1 pint vegetable stock
2 tsp sunflower oil
2 shallots, peeled and finely chopped
1 garlic clove, peeled and crushed
1 green pepper, deseeded and cut
   into small dice
1 red chilli, deseeded and
   finely chopped
50 g/2 oz button mushrooms
   finely chopped
1 tbsp freshly chopped oregano
salt and freshly ground black pepper
4 large ripe beef tomatoes
1 large egg, beaten
1 tsp caster sugar
basil leaves, to garnish
crusty bread, to serve

TASTY TIP

This dish is also delicious when made with meat. Add 125 g/4 oz of minced beef in step 2. Heat the frying pan and dry-fry the meat on a high heat until cooked through and brown, before adding the rest of the ingredients.

1 Preheat the oven to 180°C/350°F/Gas Mark 4. Place the rice in a saucepan, pour over the vegetable stock and bring to the boil. Simmer for 30 minutes or until the rice is tender. Drain and turn into a mixing bowl.

2 Add 1 teaspoon of sunflower oil to a small non-stick pan and gently fry the shallots, garlic, pepper, chilli and mushrooms for 2 minutes. Add to the rice with the chopped oregano. Season with plenty of salt and pepper.

3 Slice the top off each tomato. Cut and scoop out the flesh, removing the hard core. Pass the tomato flesh through a sieve. Add 1 tablespoon of the juice to the rice mixture. Stir in the beaten egg and mix. Sprinkle a little sugar in the base of each tomato. Pile the rice mixture into the shells.

4 Place the tomatoes in a baking dish and pour a little cold water around them. Replace their lids and drizzle a few drops of sunflower oil over the tops.

5 Bake in the preheated oven for about 25 minutes. Garnish with the basil leaves and season with black pepper and serve immediately with crusty bread.

2

3

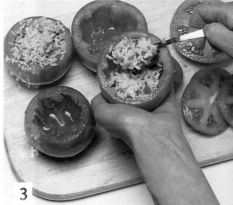

3

Stuffed Onions with Pine Nuts

INGREDIENTS

Serves 4

4 medium onions, peeled
2 garlic cloves, peeled and crushed
2 tbsp fresh brown breadcrumbs
2 tbsp white breadcrumbs
25 g/1 oz sultanas
25 g/1 oz pine nuts
50 g/2 oz low-fat hard cheese such as Edam, grated
2 tbsp freshly chopped parsley
1 medium egg, beaten
salt and freshly ground black pepper
salad leaves, to serve

1 Preheat the oven to 200°C/400°F/Gas Mark 6. Bring a pan of water to the boil, add the onions and cook gently for about 15 minutes.

2 Drain well. Allow the onions to cool, then slice each one in half horizontally.

3 Scoop out most of the onion flesh but leave a reasonably firm shell.

4 Chop up 4 tablespoons of the onion flesh and place in a bowl with the crushed garlic, breadcrumbs, sultanas, pine nuts, grated cheese and parsley.

5 Mix the breadcrumb mixture together thoroughly. Bind together with as much of the beaten egg as necessary to make a firm filling. Season to taste with salt and pepper.

6 Pile the mixture back into the onion shells and top with the grated cheese. Place on a oiled baking tray and cook in the preheated oven for 20–30 minutes or until golden brown. Serve immediately with the   salad leaves.

FOOD FACT

While this dish is delicious on its own, it also compliments barbecued meat and fish. The onion takes on a mellow, nutty flavour when baked.

3

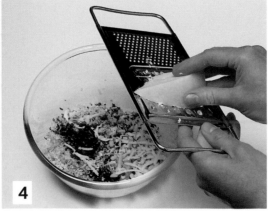

4

6

Warm Leek & Tomato Salad

INGREDIENTS

Serves 4

450 g/1 lb trimmed baby leeks
225 g/8 oz ripe but firm tomatoes
2 shallots, peeled and cut into
  thin wedges

For the honey and lime dressing:

2 tbsp clear honey
grated rind of 1 lime
4 tbsp lime juice
1 tbsp light olive oil
1 tsp Dijon mustard
salt and freshly ground black pepper

To garnish:

freshly chopped tarragon
freshly chopped basil

HELPFUL HINT

An easy way to measure honey is to plunge a metal measuring spoon into boiling water. Drain the spoon, then dip into the honey.

1   Trim the leeks so that they are all the same length. Place in a steamer over a pan of boiling water and steam for 8 minutes or until just tender.

2   Drain the leeks thoroughly and arrange in a shallow serving dish.

3   Make a cross in the top of the tomatoes, place in a bowl and cover them with boiling water until their skins start to peel away. Remove from the bowl and carefully remove the skins.

4   Cut the tomatoes into four and remove the seeds, then chop into small dice. Spoon over the top of the leeks together with the shallots.

5   In a small bowl make the dressing by whisking the honey, lime rind, lime juice, olive oil, mustard and salt and pepper. Pour 3 tablespoons of the dressing over the leeks and tomatoes and garnish with the tarragon and basil. Serve while the leeks are still warm, with the remaining dressing served separately.

1

3

5

Winter Coleslaw

INGREDIENTS

Serves 6

175 g/6 oz white cabbage

1 medium red onion, peeled

175 g/6 oz carrot, peeled

175 g/6 oz celeriac, peeled

2 celery stalks, trimmed

75 g/3 oz golden sultanas

For the yogurt & herb dressing:

150 ml/¼ pint low-fat natural yogurt

1 garlic clove, peeled and crushed

1 tbsp lemon juice

1 tsp clear honey

1 tbsp freshly snipped chives

TASTY TIP

To make cheese coleslaw, simply replace the sultanas with 75 g/3 oz of reduced-fat cheese. Whether the winter or cheese variety, coleslaw is particularly good with baked potatoes and a little low-fat spread.

1 Remove the hard core from the cabbage with a small knife and shred finely.

2 Slice the onion finely and coarsely grate the carrot.

3 Place the raw vegetables in a large bowl and mix together.

4 Cut the celeriac into thin strips and simmer in boiling water for about 2 minutes.

5 Drain the celeriac and rinse thoroughly with cold water.

6 Chop the celery and add to the bowl with the celeriac and sultanas and mix well.

7 Make the yogurt and herb dressing by briskly whisking the yogurt, garlic, lemon juice, honey and chives together.

8 Pour the dressing over the top of the salad. Stir the vegetables thoroughly to coat evenly and serve.

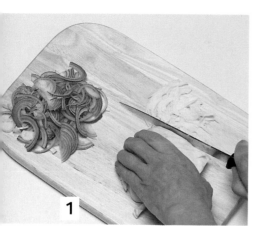
1

4

6

Mediterranean Feast

INGREDIENTS

Serves 4

1 small iceberg lettuce
225 g/8 oz French beans
225 g/8 oz baby new
　potatoes, scrubbed
4 medium eggs
1 green pepper
1 medium onion, peeled
200 g can tuna in brine, drained and
　flaked into small pieces
50 g/2 oz low-fat hard cheese, such
　as Edam, cut into small cubes
8 ripe but firm cherry
　tomatoes, quartered
50 g/2 oz black pitted olives, halved
freshly chopped basil, to garnish

For the lime vinaigrette:

3 tbsp light olive oil
2 tbsp white wine vinegar
4 tbsp lime juice
grated rind of 1 lime
1 tsp Dijon mustard
1-2 tsp caster sugar
salt and freshly ground black pepper

1　Cut the lettuce into four and remove the hard core. Tear into bite-sized pieces and arrange on a large serving platter or four individual plates.

2　Cook the French beans in boiling salted water for 8 minutes and the potatoes for 10 minutes or until tender. Drain and rinse in cold water until cool, then cut both the beans and potatoes in half with a sharp knife.

3　Boil the eggs for 10 minutes, then rinse thoroughly under a cold running tap until cool. Remove the shells under water and cut each egg into four.

4　Remove the seeds from the pepper and cut into thin strips and finely chop the onion.

5　Arrange the beans, potatoes, eggs, peppers and onion on top of the lettuce. Add the tuna, cheese and tomatoes. Sprinkle over the olives and garnish with the basil.

6　To make the vinaigrette, place all the ingredients in a screw-topped jar and shake vigorously until everything is mixed thoroughly. Spoon 4 tablespoons over the top of the prepared salad and serve the remainder separately.

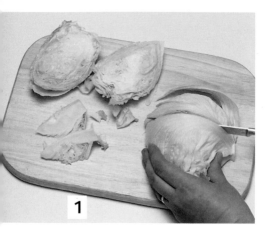

1

4

5

Beetroot & Potato Medley

INGREDIENTS

Serves 4

350 g/12 oz raw baby beetroot
½ tsp sunflower oil
225 g/8 oz new potatoes
½ cucumber, peeled
3 tbsp white wine vinegar
150 ml/5 fl oz natural low-fat yogurt
salt and freshly ground black pepper
fresh salad leaves
1 tbsp freshly snipped chives,
  to garnish

1   Preheat the oven to 180°C/350°F/Gas Mark 4. Scrub the beetroot thoroughly and place on a baking tray.

2   Brush the beetroot with a little oil and cook for 1½ hours or until a skewer is easily insertable into the beetroot. Allow to cool a little, then remove the skins.

3   Cook the potatoes in boiling water for about 10 minutes. Rinse in cold water and drain. Reserve the potatoes until cool. Dice evenly.

4   Cut the cucumber into cubes and place in a mixing bowl. Chop the beetroot into small cubes and add to the bowl with the reserved potatoes. Gently mix the vegetables together.

5   Mix together the vinegar and yogurt and season to taste with a little salt and pepper. Pour over the vegetables and combine gently.

6   Arrange on a bed of salad leaves garnished with the snipped chives and serve.

HELPFUL HINT

Beetroot can also be cooked in the microwave. Place in a microwaveable bowl. Add sufficient water to come halfway up the sides of the bowl. Cover and cook for 10–15 minutes on high. Leave for 5 minutes before removing the paper. Cook before peeling.

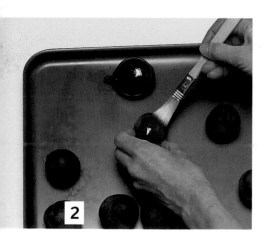

Sicilian Baked Aubergine

INGREDIENTS

Serves 4

1 large aubergine, trimmed
2 celery stalks, trimmed
4 large ripe tomatoes
1 tsp sunflower oil
2 shallots, peeled and finely chopped
1½ tsp tomato purée
25 g/1 oz green pitted olives
25 g/1 oz black pitted olives
salt and freshly ground black pepper
1 tbsp white wine vinegar
2 tsp caster sugar
1 tbsp freshly chopped basil,
   to garnish
mixed salad leaves, to serve

FOOD FACT

It has been suggested, that foods which are purple in colour, such as aubergines, have particularly powerful antioxidants, which help the body to protect itself from disease and strengthen the organs.

1 Preheat the oven to 200°C/400°F/Gas Mark 6. Cut the aubergine into small cubes and place on an oiled baking tray.

2 Cover the tray with tinfoil and bake in the preheated oven for 15–20 minutes until soft. Reserve, to allow the aubergine to cool.

3 Place the celery and tomatoes in a large bowl and cover with boiling water.

4 Remove the tomatoes from the bowl when their skins begin to peel away. Remove the skins then, deseed and chop the flesh into small pieces.

5 Remove the celery from the bowl of water, finely chop and reserve.

6 Pour the vegetable oil into a non-stick saucepan, add the chopped shallots and fry gently for 2–3 minutes until soft. Add the celery, tomatoes, tomato purée and olives. Season to taste with salt and pepper.

7 Simmer gently for 3–4 minutes. Add the vinegar, sugar and cooled aubergine to the pan and heat gently for 2–3 minutes until all the ingredients are well blended. Reserve to allow the aubergine mixture to cool. When cool, garnish with the chopped basil and serve cold with salad leaves.

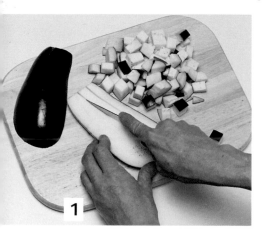
1

5

6

Carrot, Celeriac & Sesame Seed Salad

INGREDIENTS

Serves 6

225 g/8 oz celeriac
225 g/8 oz carrots, peeled
50 g/2 oz seedless raisins
2 tbsp sesame seeds
freshly chopped parsley,
   to garnish

For the lemon & chilli dressing:

grated rind of 1 lemon
4 tbsp lemon juice
2 tbsp sunflower oil
2 tbsp clear honey
1 red bird's eye chilli, deseeded and
   finely chopped
salt and freshly ground black pepper

1   Slice the celeriac into thin matchsticks. Place in a small saucepan of boiling salted water and boil for 2 minutes.

2   Drain and rinse the celeriac in cold water and place in a mixing bowl.

3   Finely grate the carrot. Add the carrot and the raisins to the celeriac in the bowl.

4   Place the sesame seeds under a hot grill or dry-fry in a frying pan for 1–2 minutes until golden brown, then leave to cool.

5   Make the dressing by whisking together the lemon rind, lemon juice, oil, honey, chilli and seasoning or by shaking thoroughly in a screw-topped jar.

6   Pour 2 tablespoons of the dressing over the salad and toss well. Turn into a serving dish and sprinkle over the toasted sesame seeds and chopped parsley. Serve the remaining dressing separately.

FOOD FACT

Celeriac is a root vegetable that is similar in taste to fennel, but with a texture closer to parsnip. This versatile vegetable has a creamy taste and is also delicious in soups and gratins.

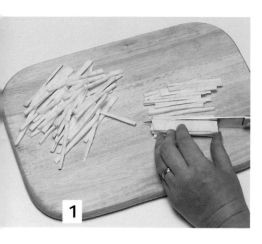

Carrot & Ginger Soup

INGREDIENTS

Serves 4

4 slices of bread, crusts removed
1 tsp yeast extract
2 tsp olive oil
1 onion, peeled and chopped
1 garlic clove, peeled
  and crushed
½ tsp ground ginger
450 g/1 lb carrots, peeled
  and chopped
1 litre/1¾ pint vegetable stock
2.5 cm/1 inch piece of root ginger,
  peeled and finely grated
salt and freshly ground black pepper
1 tbsp lemon juice

To garnish:

chives
lemon zest

TASTY TIP

Serve with slices of bruschetta, which can be easily made by lightly grilling thick slices of ciabatta bread on both sides. While still warm, rub with a whole, peeled clove of garlic and drizzle with a little good quality extra virgin olive oil.

1 Preheat the oven to 180°C/350°F/Gas Mark 4. Roughly chop the bread. Dissolve the yeast extract in 2 tablespoons of warm water and mix with the bread.

2 Spread the bread cubes over a lightly oiled baking tray and bake for 20 minutes, turning half way through. Remove from the oven and reserve.

3 Heat the oil in a large saucepan. Gently cook the onion and garlic for 3–4 minutes.

4 Stir in the ground ginger and cook for 1 minute to release the flavour.

5 Add the chopped carrots, then stir in the stock and the fresh ginger. Simmer gently for 15 minutes.

6 Remove from the heat and allow to cool a little. Blend until smooth, then season to taste with salt and pepper. Stir in the lemon juice. Garnish with the chives and lemon zest and serve immediately.

2

4

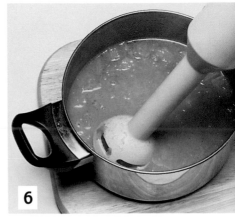

6

Roasted Red Pepper, Tomato & Red Onion Soup

INGREDIENTS

Serves 4

fine spray of oil
2 large red peppers, deseeded
   and roughly chopped
1 red onion, peeled and
   roughly chopped
350 g/12 oz tomatoes, halved
1 small crusty French loaf
1 garlic clove, peeled
600 ml/1 pint vegetable stock
salt and freshly ground black pepper
1 tsp Worcestershire sauce
4 tbsp half-fat fromage frais

HELPFUL HINT

A quick, hassle-free way to remove the skin from peppers once they have been roasted or grilled is to place them in a polythene bag. Leave for 10 minutes or until cool enough to handle, then simply peel the skin away from the flesh.

1 Preheat the oven to 190°C/375°F/Gas Mark 5. Spray a large roasting tin with the oil and place the peppers and onion in the base. Cook in the oven for 10 minutes. Add the tomatoes and cook for a further 20 minutes or until the peppers are soft.

2 Cut the bread into 1 cm/½ inch slices. Cut the garlic clove in half and rub the cut edge of the garlic over the bread.

3 Place all the bread slices on a large baking tray, and bake in the preheated oven for 10 minutes, turning halfway through, until golden and crisp.

4 Remove the vegetables from the oven and allow to cool slightly, then blend in a food processor until smooth. Strain the vegetable mixture through a large nylon sieve into a saucepan, to remove the seeds and skin. Add the stock, season to taste with salt and pepper and stir to mix. Heat the soup gently until piping hot.

5 In a small bowl beat together the Worcestershire sauce with the fromage frais.

6 Pour the soup into warmed bowls and swirl a spoonful of the fromage frais mixture into each bowl. Serve immediately with the garlic toasts.

Orange Freeze

INGREDIENTS

Serves 4

4 large oranges
about 300 ml/½ pint low-fat
   vanilla ice cream
225 g/8 oz raspberries
75 g/3 oz icing sugar, sifted
redcurrant sprigs, to decorate

TASTY TIP

The fresh citrus in this dish works to clear the palate. The acidity combines well with the creaminess of the ice cream. Orange is very good with mango, so why not experiment by adding the flesh of a small ripe mango in step 4 for a more fragrant dessert? Lemons would also work well in this recipe.

1 Set the freezer to rapid freeze. Using a sharp knife carefully cut the lid off each orange.

2 Scoop out the flesh from the orange, discarding any pips and thick pith.

3 Place the shells and lids in the freezer and chop any remaining orange flesh.

4 Whisk together the orange juice, orange flesh and vanilla ice cream, until well blended.

5 Cover and freeze, for about 2 hours, occasionally breaking up the ice crystals with a fork or a whisk. Stir the mixture from around the edge of the container into the centre, then level and return to the freezer. Do this 2–3 times then leave until almost frozen solid.

6 Place a large scoop of the ice cream mixture into the frozen shells. Add another scoop on top, so that there is plenty outside of the orange shell and return to the freezer for 1 hour.

7 Arrange the lids on top and freeze for a further 2 hours, until the filled orange shell is completely frozen solid.

8 Meanwhile, using a nylon sieve press the raspberries into a bowl using the back of a wooden spoon and mix together with the icing sugar. Spoon the raspberry coulis on to four serving plates and place an orange at the centre of each. Dust with icing sugar and serve decorated with the redcurrants. Remember to return the freezer to its normal setting.

2

5

8

Rice Pudding

INGREDIENTS

Serves 4

60 g/2½ oz pudding rice
50 g/2 oz granulated sugar
410 g can light evaporated milk
300 ml/½ pint semi-skimmed milk
pinch of freshly
grated nutmeg
25 g/1 oz half-fat butter
reduced sugar jam, to decorate

TASTY TIP

Traditionally, rice pudding was cooked alongside the Sunday roast which, after many hours in the oven, came out rich and creamy. The main trick to achieving traditional creamy rice pudding is not using cream and full-fat milk, but instead long, slow cooking on a low temperature. Try adding a few sultanas and lemon peel, or a few roughly crushed cardamom pods for an alternative flavour. It is also delicious dusted with a little ground cinnamon.

1 Preheat the oven to 150°C/300°F/Gas Mark 2. Lightly oil a large ovenproof dish.

2 Sprinkle the rice and the sugar into the dish and mix.

3 Bring the evaporated milk and milk to the boil in a small pan, stirring occasionally.

4 Stir the milks into the rice and mix well until the rice is coated thoroughly.

5 Sprinkle over the nutmeg, cover with tinfoil and bake in the preheated oven for 30 minutes.

6 Remove the pudding from the oven and stir well, breaking up any lumps.

7 Cover with the same tinfoil. Bake in the preheated oven for a further 30 minutes. Remove from the oven and stir well again.

8 Dot the pudding with butter and bake for a further 45–60 minutes, until the rice is tender and the skin is browned.

9 Divide the pudding into four individual serving bowls. Top with a large spoonful of the jam and serve immediately.

2

4

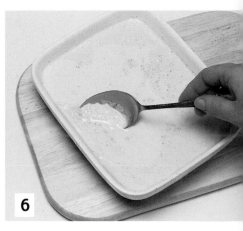

6

Orange Curd & Plum Puddings

INGREDIENTS

Serves 4

700 g/1½ lb plums, stoned
  and quartered
2 tbsp light brown sugar
grated rind of ½ lemon
25 g/1 oz butter, melted
1 tbsp olive oil
6 sheets filo pastry
½ x 411 g jar luxury orange curd
50 g/2 oz sultanas
icing sugar, to decorate
half-fat thick-set Greek yogurt,
  to serve

1 Preheat the oven to 200°C/400°F/Gas Mark 6. Lightly oil a 20.5 cm/8 inch round cake tin. Cook the plums with 2 tablespoons of the light brown sugar for 8–10 minutes to soften them, remove from the heat and reserve.

2 Mix together the lemon rind, butter and oil. Lay a sheet of pastry in the prepared cake tin and brush with the lemon rind mixture.

3 Cut the sheets of filo pastry in half and then place one half sheet in the cake tin and brush again.

4 Top with the remaining halved sheets of pastry brushing each time with the lemon rind mixture. Fold each sheet in half lengthwise to line the sides of the tin to make a filo case.

5 Mix together the plums, orange curd and sultanas and spoon into the pastry case.

6 Draw the pastry edges up over the filling to enclose. Brush the remaining sheets of filo pastry with the lemon rind mixture and cut into thick strips.

7 Scrunch each strip of pastry and arrange on top of the pie. Bake in the preheated oven for 25 minutes, until golden. Sprinkle with icing sugar and serve with the Greek yogurt.

2

5

7

Sweet–stewed Dried Fruits

INGREDIENTS

Serves 4

500 g/1 lb 2 oz packet mixed dried
   fruit salad
450 ml/¾ pint apple juice
2 tbsp clear honey
2 tbsp brandy
1 lemon
1 orange

To decorate:

half-fat crème fraîche
fine strips of pared orange rind

TASTY TIP

As a dessert, this dish is particularly good when served with cold rice pudding. However, these stewed fruits can also be very nice for breakfast. Simply pour some unsweetened muesli into the bottom of a bowl, top with the stewed fruits and perhaps some low-fat natural yogurt and serve.

1 Place the fruits, apple juice, clear honey and brandy in a small saucepan.

2 Using a small, sharp knife or a zester, carefully remove the zest from the lemon and orange and place in the pan.

3 Squeeze the juice from the lemon and oranges and add to the pan.

4 Bring the fruit mixture to the boil and simmer for about 1 minute. Remove the pan from the heat and allow the mixture to cool completely.

5 Transfer the mixture to a large bowl, cover with clingfilm and chill in the refrigerator overnight to allow the flavours to blend.

6 Spoon the stewed fruit in four shallow dessert dishes. Decorate with a large spoonful of half-fat crème fraîche and a few strips of the pared orange rind and serve.

2

3

4

Autumn Fruit Layer

INGREDIENTS

Serves 4

450 g/1 lb Bramley cooking apples
225 g/8 oz blackberries
50 g/2 oz soft brown sugar
juice of 1 lemon
50 g/2 oz low-fat spread
200 g/7 oz breadcrumbs
225 g/8 oz honey-coated nut
  mix, chopped
redcurrants and mint leaves,
  to decorate
half-fat whipped cream or reduced-fat
  ice cream, to serve

TASTY TIP

Any autumn fruit can be used in this recipe. Add pear to this recipe to make an apple and pear fruit layer or use some plums if preferred. For a more textured pudding, reduce the amount of breadcrumbs used to 150 g/5 oz and add 50 g/2 oz of rolled oats in step 5.

1 Peel, core and slice the cooking apples and place in a saucepan with the blackberries, sugar and lemon juice.

2 Cover the fruit mixture and simmer, stirring occasionally for about 15 minutes or until the apples and blackberries have formed into a thick purée.

3 Remove the pan from the heat and allow to cool.

4 Melt the low-fat spread in a frying pan and cook the breadcrumbs for 5–10 minutes, stirring occasionally until golden and crisp.

5 Remove the pan from the heat and stir in the nuts. Allow to cool.

6 Alternately layer the fruit purée and breadcrumbs into four tall glasses.

7 Store the desserts in the refrigerator to chill and remove when ready to serve.

8 Decorate with redcurrants and mint leaves and serve with half-fat whipped cream or a reduced-fat vanilla or raspberry ice cream.

1

4

6

Oaty Fruit Puddings

INGREDIENTS

Serves 4

125 g/4 oz rolled oats
50 g/2 oz low-fat
  spread, melted
2 tbsp chopped almonds
1 tbsp clear honey
pinch of ground cinnamon
2 pears, peeled, cored and
  finely chopped
1 tbsp marmalade
orange zest, to decorate
low-fat custard or fruit-flavoured
  low-fat yogurt, to serve

TASTY TIP

Liqueur custard is superb with steamed and baked puddings. Add 2–3 tablespoons of either Cointreau or a liqueur of your choice to the custard, together with 1 teaspoon of vanilla essence. Taste the custard and add more alcohol if desired.

1. Preheat the oven to 200°C/400°F/Gas Mark 6. Lightly oil and line the bases of four individual pudding bowls or muffin tins with a small circle of greaseproof paper.

2. Mix together the oats, low-fat spread, nuts, honey and cinnamon in a small bowl.

3. Using a spoon, spread two thirds of the oaty mixture over the base and around the sides of the pudding bowls or muffin tins.

4. Toss together the pears and marmalade and spoon into the oaty cases.

5. Scatter over the remaining oaty mixture to cover the pears and marmalade.

6. Bake in the preheated oven for 15–20 minutes, until cooked and the tops of the puddings are golden and crisp.

7. Leave for 5 minutes before removing the pudding bowls or the muffin tins. Decorate with orange zest and serve hot with low-fat custard or low-fat fruit-flavoured yogurt.

1

3

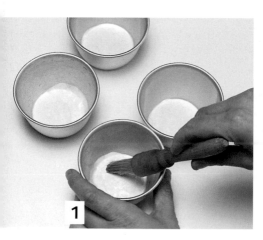

4

Fruit Salad

INGREDIENTS

Serves 4

125 g/4 oz caster sugar
3 oranges
700 g/1½ lb lychees,
   peeled and stoned
1 small mango
1 small pineapple
1 papaya
4 pieces stem ginger in syrup
4 tbsp stem ginger syrup
125 g/4 oz Cape gooseberries
125 g/4 oz strawberries, hulled
½ tsp almond essence

To decorate:

lime zest
mint leaves

FOOD FACT

A fruit salad is the perfect end to a good meal because it refreshes the palate and is also packed full of vitamins.

1 Place the sugar and 300 ml/½ pint of water in a small pan and heat, gently stirring until the sugar has dissolved. Bring to the boil and simmer for 2 minutes. Once a syrup has formed, remove from the heat and allow to cool.

2 Using a sharp knife, cut away the skin from the oranges, then slice thickly. Cut each slice in half and place in a serving dish with the syrup and lychees.

3 Peel the mango, then cut into thick slices around each side of the stone. Discard the stone and cut the slices into bite-sized pieces and add to the syrup.

4 Using a sharp knife again, carefully cut away the skin from the pineapple.

5 Remove the central core using the knife or an apple corer, then cut the pineapple into segments and add to the syrup.

6 Peel the papaya, then cut in half and remove the seeds. Cut the flesh into chunks, slice the ginger into matchsticks and add with the ginger syrup to the fruit in the syrup.

7 Prepare the Cape gooseberries, by removing the thin, papery skins and rinsing lightly.

8 Halve the strawberries, add to the fruit with the almond essence and chill for 30 minutes. Scatter with mint leaves and lime zest to decorate and serve.

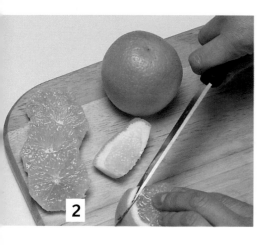

2

3

4

Summer Pavlova

INGREDIENTS

Serves 4

4 medium egg whites
225 g/8 oz caster sugar
1 tsp vanilla essence
2 tsp white wine vinegar
1½ tsp cornflour
300 ml/½ pint half-fat Greek yogurt
2 tbsp honey
225 g/8 oz strawberries, hulled
125 g/4 oz raspberries
125 g/4 oz blueberries
4 kiwis, peeled and sliced
icing sugar, to decorate

HELPFUL HINT

Always remember to double check that the bowl being used to whisk egg whites is completely clean, as you will find that any grease will prevent the egg whites from rising into the stiff consistency necessary for this recipe.

1 Preheat the oven to 150°C/300°F/Gas Mark 2. Line a baking sheet with a sheet of greaseproof or baking parchment paper.

2 Place the egg whites in a clean grease-free bowl and whisk until very stiff.

3 Whisk in half the sugar, vanilla essence, vinegar and cornflour and continue whisking until stiff.

4 Gradually, whisk in the remaining sugar, a teaspoonful at a time until very stiff and glossy.

5 Using a large spoon, arrange spoonfuls of the meringue in a circle on the greaseproof paper or baking parchment paper.

6 Bake in the preheated oven for 1 hour until crisp and dry. Turn the oven off and leave the meringue in the oven to cool completely.

7 Remove the meringue from the baking sheet and peel away the parchment paper. Mix together the yogurt and honey. Place the pavlova on a serving plate and spoon the yogurt into the centre.

8 Scatter over the strawberries, raspberries, blueberries and kiwis. Dust with the icing sugar and serve.

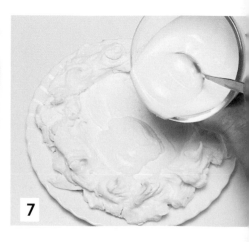

Poached Pears

INGREDIENTS

Serves 4

2 small cinnamon sticks
125 g/4 oz caster sugar
300 ml/½ pint red wine
150 ml/¼ pint water
thinly pared rind and juice of
　1 small orange
4 firm pears
orange slices, to decorate
frozen vanilla yogurt, or
　low-fat ice cream, to serve

TASTY TIP

Poached pears are delicious served with a little half-fat crème fraîche and sprinkled with toasted almonds. To toast almonds, simply warm the grill and place whole, blanched almonds or flaked almonds on to a piece of tinfoil. Place under the grill and toast lightly on both sides for 1–2 minutes until golden. Remove and cool, chop if liked.

1　Place the cinnamon sticks on the work surface and with a rolling pin, slowly roll down the side of the cinnamon stick to bruise. Place in a large heavy-based saucepan.

2　Add the sugar, wine, water, pared orange rind and juice to the pan and bring slowly to the boil, stirring occasionally, until the sugar is dissolved.

3　Meanwhile peel the pears, leaving the stalks on.

4　Cut out the cores from the bottom of the pears and level them so that they stand upright.

5　Stand the pears in the syrup, cover the pan and simmer for 20 minutes or until tender.

6　Remove the pan from the heat and leave the pears to cool in the syrup, turning occasionally.

7　Arrange the pears on serving plates and spoon over the syrup. Decorate with the orange slices and serve with the yogurt or low-fat ice cream and any remaining juices.

1

2

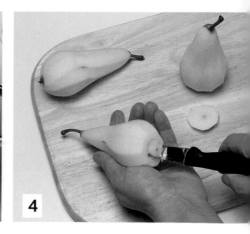

4

Grape & Almond Layer

INGREDIENTS

Serves 4

300 ml/½ pint low-fat fromage frais
300 ml/½ pint half-fat Greek yogurt
3 tbsp icing sugar, sifted
2 tbsp crème de cassis
450 g/1 lb red grapes
175 g/6 oz Amaretti biscuits
2 ripe passion fruit

To decorate:
icing sugar
extra grapes, optional

1 Mix together the fromage frais and yogurt in a bowl and lightly fold in the sifted icing sugar and crème de cassis with a large metal spoon or rubber spatula until lightly blended.

2 Using a small knife, remove the seeds from the grapes if necessary. Rinse lightly and pat dry on absorbent kitchen paper.

3 Place the deseeded grapes in a bowl and stir in any juice from the grapes from deseeding.

4 Place the Amaretti biscuits in a polythene bag and crush roughly with a rolling pin. (Alternatively, use a food processor.)

5 Cut the passion fruit in half, scoop out the seeds with a teaspoon and reserve.

6 Divide the yogurt mixture between four tall glasses, then layer alternately with grapes, crushed biscuits and most of the passion fruit seeds. Top with the yogurt mixture and the remaining passion fruit seeds. Chill for 1 hour and decorate with extra grapes. Lightly dust with icing sugar and serve.

FOOD FACT

Passion fruits are native to Brazil. They are purple in colour and are about the size of an egg. Look for fruits that are wrinkled, not smooth. When wrinkled they are ripe and at their best.

1

2

5

Summer Pudding

INGREDIENTS

Serves 4

450 g/1 lb redcurrants
125 g/4 oz caster sugar
350 g/12 oz strawberries, hulled
  and halved
125 g/4 oz raspberries
2 tbsp Grand Marnier or Cointreau
8–10 medium slices white bread,
  crusts removed
mint sprigs, to decorate
low-fat Greek yogurt or
  low-fat fromage frais, to serve

TASTY TIP

This really is a summer pudding, using plump, juicy berries that are bursting with flavour. Why not try an autumn version using seasonal fruit such as blackberries, plums and flavoursome apples? Place in just a few tablespoons of water, together with 50 g/2 oz of caster sugar and heat gently as in step 1.

1 Place the redcurrants, sugar and 1 tablespoon of water in a large saucepan. Heat gently until the sugar has just dissolved and the juices have just begun to run.

2 Remove the saucepan from the heat and stir in the strawberries, raspberries and the Grand Marnier or Cointreau.

3 Line the base and sides of a 1.1 litre/2 pint pudding basin with two thirds of the bread, making sure that the slices overlap each other slightly.

4 Spoon the fruit with their juices into the bread-lined pudding basin, then top with the remaining bread slices.

5 Place a small plate on top of the pudding inside the pudding basin. Ensure the plate fits tightly, then weigh down with a clean can or some weights and chill in the refrigerator overnight.

6 When ready to serve, remove the weights and plate. Carefully loosen round the sides of the basin with a round-bladed knife. Invert the pudding on to a serving plate, decorate with the mint sprigs and serve with the yogurt or fromage frais.

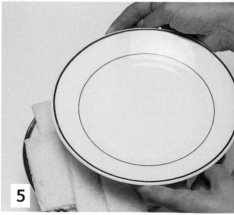

Caramelised Oranges in an Iced Bowl

INGREDIENTS

Serves 4

For the ice bowl:

about 36 ice cubes
fresh flowers and fruits
8 medium-sized oranges
225 g/8 oz caster sugar
4 tbsp Grand Marnier or Cointreau

1 Set freezer to rapid freeze. Place a few ice cubes in the base of a 1.7 litre/3 pint freezable glass bowl. Place a 900 ml/1½ pint glass bowl on top of the ice cubes. Arrange the flower heads and fruits in between the 2 bowls, wedging in position with the ice cubes.

2 Weigh down the smaller bowl with some heavy weights, then carefully pour cold water between the 2 bowls making sure that the flowers and the fruit are covered. Freeze for at least 6 hours or until the ice is frozen solid.

3 When ready to use, remove the weights and using a hot damp cloth rub the inside of the smaller bowl with the cloth until it loosens sufficiently for you to remove the bowl. Place the larger bowl in the sink or washing-up bowl, half filled with very hot water. Leave for about 30 seconds or until the ice loosens. Take care not to leave the bowl in the water for too long otherwise the ice will melt. Remove the bowl and leave in the refrigerator. Return the freezer to its normal setting.

4 Thinly pare the rind from 2 oranges and then cut into julienne strips. Using a sharp knife cut away the rind and pith from all the oranges, holding over a bowl to catch the juices. Slice the oranges, discarding any pips and reform each orange back to its original shape. Secure with cocktail sticks, then place in a bowl.

5 Heat 300 ml/½ pint water, orange rind and sugar together in a pan. Stir the sugar until dissolved. Bring to the boil. Boil for 15 minutes, until it is a caramel colour. Remove pan from heat.

HELPFUL HINT

This iced bowl can hold any dessert. Why not fill with flavoured ice creams?

6 Stir in the liqueur, pour over the oranges. Allow to cool. Chill for 3 hours, turning the oranges occasionally. Spoon into the ice bowl and serve.

1

2

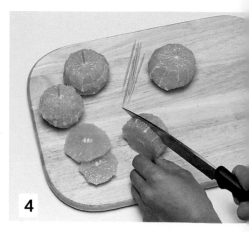
4

Raspberry Sorbet Crush

INGREDIENTS

Serves 4

225 g/8 oz raspberries, thawed
  if frozen
grated rind and juice of 1 lime
300 ml/½ pint orange juice
225 g/8 oz caster sugar
2 medium egg whites

FOOD FACT

This recipe contains raw egg and should not be given to babies, young children, pregnant women, the sick, the elderly and those suffering from a recurring illness.

1 Set the freezer to rapid freeze. If using fresh raspberries pick over and lightly rinse.

2 Place the raspberries in a dish and, using a masher, mash to a chunky purée.

3 Place the lime rind and juice, orange juice and half the caster sugar in a large heavy-based saucepan.

4 Heat gently stirring frequently until the sugar is dissolved. Bring to the boil and boil rapidly for about 5 minutes.

5 Remove the pan from the heat and pour carefully into a freezable container.

6 Leave to cool, then place in the freezer and freeze for 2 hours, stirring occasionally to break up the ice crystals.

7 Fold the ice mixture into the raspberry purée with a metal spoon and freeze for a further 2 hours, stirring occasionally.

8 Whisk the egg whites until stiff. Then gradually whisk in the remaining caster sugar a tablespoon at a time until the egg white mixture is stiff and glossy.

9 Fold into the raspberry sorbet with a metal spoon and freeze for 1 hour. Spoon into tall glasses and serve immediately. Remember to return the freezer to its normal setting.

2

7

9

Raspberry Soufflé

INGREDIENTS

Serves 4

125 g/4 oz redcurrants
50 g/2 oz caster sugar
1 sachet (3 tsp) powdered gelatine
3 medium eggs, separated
300 g/½ pint half-fat Greek yogurt
450 g/1 lb raspberries, thawed
  if frozen

To decorate:

mint sprigs
extra fruits

HELPFUL HINT

Soufflés rely on air, so it is important that the egg whites in this recipe are beaten until very stiff in order to support the other mixture.

1 Wrap a band of double thickness greaseproof paper around four ramekin dishes, making sure that 5 cm/2 inches of the paper stays above the top of each dish. Secure the paper to the dish with an elastic band or Sellotape.

2 Place the redcurrants and 1 tablespoon of the sugar in a small saucepan. Cook for 5 minutes until softened. Remove from the heat, sieve and reserve.

3 Place 3 tablespoons of water in a small bowl and sprinkle over the gelatine. Allow to stand for 5 minutes until spongy. Place the bowl over a pan of simmering water and leave until dissolved. Remove and allow to cool.

4 Beat together the remaining sugar and egg yolks until pale thick and creamy, then fold in the yogurt with a metal spoon or rubber spatula until well blended.

5 Sieve the raspberries and fold into the yogurt mixture with the gelatine. Whisk the egg whites until stiff and fold into the yogurt mixture. Pour into the prepared dishes and chill in the refrigerator for 2 hours until firm.

6 Remove the paper from the dishes and spread the redcurrant purée over the top of the soufflés. Decorate with mint sprigs and extra fruits and serve.

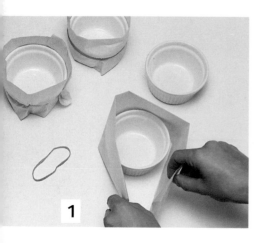

1

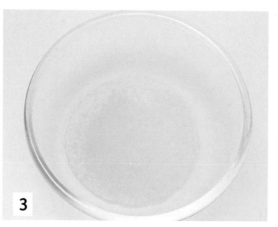

3

5

Fruity Roulade

INGREDIENTS

Serves 4

For the sponge:

3 medium eggs
75 g/3 oz caster sugar
75 g/3 oz plain flour, sieved
1–2 tbsp caster sugar for sprinkling

For the filling:

125 g/4 oz Quark
125 g/4 oz half-fat Greek yogurt
25 g/1 oz caster sugar
1 tbsp orange liqueur (optional)
grated rind of 1 orange
125 g/4 oz strawberries, hulled and
  cut into quarters

To decorate:

strawberries
sifted icing sugar

FOOD FACT

Quark is a soft unripened cheese with the flavour and texture of soured cream. It comes in 2 varieties, low fat and non-fat. Quark can be used as a sour cream substitute to top baked potatoes, or in dips and cheesecakes.

1. Preheat the oven to 220°C/425°F/Gas Mark 7. Lightly oil and line a 33 x 23 cm/13 x 9 inch Swiss roll tin with greaseproof or baking parchment paper.

2. Using an electric whisk, whisk the eggs and sugar until the mixture is double in volume and leaves a trail across the top.

3. Fold in the flour with a metal spoon or rubber spatula. Pour into the prepared tin and bake in the preheated oven for 10–12 minutes, until well risen and golden.

4. Place a whole sheet of greaseproof or baking parchment paper out on a flat work surface and sprinkle evenly with caster sugar.

5. Turn the cooked sponge out on to the paper, discard the paper, trim the sponge and roll up encasing the paper inside. Reserve until cool.

6. To make the filling, mix together the Quark, yogurt, caster sugar, liqueur (if using) and orange rind. Unroll the roulade and spread over the mixture. Scatter over the strawberries and roll up.

7. Decorate the roulade with the strawberries. Dust with the icing sugar and serve.

2

5

6

Index